THE DISCIPLINE
of DELUSION:

How Secular Ideas Became the New Idolatry

by

Jerry Bangert

THE DISCIPLINE
of DELUSION

Illumify Media Group
www.IllumifyMedia.com
"We Make Your Writing Shine"

Paperback ISBN: 978-1-947360-04-4
eBook ISBN: 978-1-947360-05-1

Printed in the United States of America
16 17 18 19 20 21 LSI 9 8 7 6 5 4 3 2 1

CONTENTS

Introduction   5

1. Purpose   15
2. God, Knowledge, and Morality   29
3. The Discipline of Delusion   46
4. The Church and Ideology   66
5. The Church and Science   90
6. The Church and Secularism   112
7. The Church and Cultural Marxism   133
8. The Importance of the Apostles   159

Conclusion   183

Endnotes   192

Introduction

IMAGINE YOURSELF AS a Christian walking the streets of second-century Rome with your family. You pass a temple dedicated to an idol when one of your children stops and asks you about it. You warn your children, "That's an idol's temple. Don't go in there. It's dangerous."

It's every Christian parent's dream! God has just given you an opportunity to teach your children the difference between Christ and pagan idolatry, between the tenets of Christianity and those of paganism.

But today in the West there are no pagan temples to warn our children to avoid. Nevertheless, idolatry is just as much a threat to our souls as it was to the early church. But it comes in a different form—the form of ideas. These ideas have invaded our schools, our entertainment, our churches and our homes without most of us being aware of the assault. How, then, can we warn our children of the evil when we don't understand it ourselves?

In the aftermath of one key event, a shift occurred in the American culture that shaped the face of idolatry for the modern American church. I vividly recall standing in the cafeteria line with my fellow eighth graders when a teacher announced that the president had been killed. As immature 13-year-olds, we tried to make light of it with graveyard humor, joking that perhaps a Republican had done it. But our forced levity could not lessen the impact of the event.

The year was 1963, and President Kennedy had just been assassinated. Just as my children remember vividly where they were on 9/11, and my parents when Pearl Harbor was bombed, I will never forget where I was on that day.

Though I don't know how, I knew that something profound had changed in our country that day. And by 1970, the country of my early childhood had vanished and was no longer recognizable to me.

The Aftermath of President Kennedy's Assassination Triggered a Moral Collapse in America

I grew up in a culture permeated by authority, which makes it difficult to describe how different it was from today. In my tiny South Dakota town, every husband was the head of his home, children obeyed their parents, teachers were in charge of their classrooms, and policemen and the government were respected. While in sixth grade, I got into an argument with my teacher. Even before my parents found out, I knew they would side with her, and sure enough, they made me apologize. Pregnancy out of wedlock was both scandalous and rare. Sexuality was a private affair, and even promiscuous Hollywood promoted a morality that by today's standard seems prudish and hypocritical.

But by 1970, just seven short years after that fateful day, all of this had been swept away. Respect for authority was not only lost but despised, as students revolted on college campuses, denouncing their professors and claiming equal or superior standing with them. Young people held government and police in contempt. Children became defiant toward their parents, and women began usurping their husband's authority not only in the marketplace but in their homes. This disdain for authority was accompanied by a disdain for traditional morality. The unapologetically wanton pursuits of pleasure in the form of sex and drugs was now rampant. And yet by today's standards, 1970 seems positively puritanical because the descent into the abyss has continued and accelerated.

I am certainly not the only one to note these changes. In his 1992 book, *Why Johnny Can't Tell Right from Wrong: Moral Illiteracy and the Case for Character Education*, William Kilpatrick cites an excellent example of this moral decay in the top concerns teachers shared about their students in 1940 compared to 1990 (in order of greatest concern).[1]

Top Concerns of Teachers in 1940:	Top Concerns of Teachers in 1990:
1. Talking out of turn	1. Drug abuse
2. Chewing gum	2. Alcohol abuse
3. Making noise	3. Pregnancy
4. Running in the halls	4. Suicide
5. Getting out of line	5. Rape
6. Wearing improper clothes	6. Robbery
7. Not putting paper in the wastebasket	7. Assault

I do not intend to idealize the '40s, '50s, and '60s. During this era, our country permitted many egregious injustices that demanded correction, and to our deep shame and the harm of many, we long neglected this moral obligation. But though the last several decades have brought improvements in these past errors, they have introduced other dramatic changes to the morality of our people as well, most of which have not been for our betterment.

Although I unconsciously recognized it as a watershed moment in American history, it was not until I encountered a 2013 article in the *Washington Post* by George Will that I finally understood the connection between the Kennedy assassination and the cultural upheaval that followed. His article, "When Liberals Became Scolds," was inspired by James Piereson's 2007 book, *Camelot and the Cultural Revolution: How the Assassination of John F. Kennedy*

Shattered American Liberalism. In his editorial, Will argues,

> The bullets of Nov. 22, 1963, altered the nation's trajectory less by killing a president than by giving birth to a destructive narrative about America . . . [and by] shatter[ing] the social consensus that characterized the 1950s only because powerful new forces of an adversarial culture were about to erupt through society's crust.[2]

In other words, the *narrative told* about the assassination rather than the *event itself,* inaugurated a new era in the United States, an era in which narrative trumped reality and the old social consensus about American morality and traditional authority structures would begin to be challenged. As Will wrote,

> The transformation of a murder by a marginal man into a killing by a sick culture began instantly —before Kennedy was buried. The afternoon of the assassination, Chief Justice Earl Warren ascribed Kennedy's "martyrdom" to "the hatred and bitterness that has been injected into the life of our nation by bigots." The next day, James Reston, the New York Times luminary, wrote in a front-page story that Kennedy was a victim of a "streak of violence in the American character,"

noting especially "the violence of the extremists on the right." Never mind that adjacent to Reston's article was a *Times* report on Oswald's Communist convictions and associations.[3]

The event so shattered the American consciousness that meaning needed to be ascribed to the event. The fact that Lee Harvey Oswald, the murderer of their beloved president, was a communist did not fit the Marxist-inspired humanistic ideology of the new intellectuals. Although the romantic narrative about Kennedy's death due to American moral decay and right-wing extremism was a lie, much of the country knowingly embraced it. Kennedy's assassination became a turning point for America because from that day on, the humanistic intellectual class bent on transforming the culture began lying to the country, and we began believing those lies.

Biblical Authority and Morality Have Been Destroyed

What began as a lie about Kennedy's assassination would continue as a lie about the country's religious and moral framework. The United States was formed by two great systems of thought: the Enlightenment and Christianity. After Kennedy's assassination, orthodox Christianity came under attack and the ideas of the Enlightenment and post-Enlightenment assumed center stage. Christianity is based on the wisdom of God; the Enlightenment on the wisdom of man. Increasingly, as

Christianity was attacked and marginalized, the wisdom of man began to rule unfettered over Christianity. As a result, biblical authority and Christian morality have been destroyed.

I certainly did not write this book to advocate a return to 1950s America. Much was wrong with the nation then, and some of the changes were long overdue and have improved the lot of many. Nor is my intent to promote a particular political creed or philosophy—I believe neither the problem nor the solution is political. Spiritual problems do not lend themselves to political solutions. Further, my concern is less for the nation (though I love my country dearly) than for the church and how Western culture has influenced and polluted it. Finally, I do not intend to imply that the ideas of the 1960s and '70s introduced anything new. Rather, they are ideas as old as the Garden of Eden.

Authority is the central issue of the Bible. The Garden of Eden is particularly instructive because it clearly lays out man's chief problem with God. In Genesis 2, God commanded Adam, "You shall not eat" from the Tree of the Knowledge of Good and Evil (verse 17). With this prohibition, God declared that He alone must define the two key elements of truth: knowledge (what is true) and morality (what is good). Since the Fall, the human race has continued to seek the autonomy to define knowledge and morality for itself. And all of history has been an unfolding of this disastrous rebellion.

Yet God in His grace chose to reassert the link between these two key areas of truth and Himself through His revelation, first with the Law and later with the commandments of Jesus and His apostles. But like Adam, the Old Testament Israelites repeatedly rejected God's authority to define these issues, instead turning to the idols of the surrounding nations. For this God judged them. Their idolatry was syncretistic; that is, they worshipped Yahweh *and* the idol rather than rejecting Yahweh and replacing Him with the idol. Jeremiah called this practice a "discipline of delusion" (Jeremiah 10:8). This syncretism led them into a delusion that they were still worshipping God when they were in fact worshipping idols.

Christians Now Worship the Idol of Ideas

It is my contention that idolatry has similarly seduced and deluded the church, but unlike Israel's idolatry, ours has taken the form of fusing the wisdom of the world (philosophy) with the wisdom of God (the Bible). This fusion began early in church history, when the church incorporated the ideas of Greek philosophy into its theology, beginning with Clement, Origen, and Augustine and later with Aquinas (among many others). Though these ideas were intended to supplement and support Christian theology, this syncretism incorporated the core ideal of Greek philosophy, the supremacy of human reason, into Christian thought. To quote Protagoras, "Man is the measure of all things." This core idea, like the Israelite's idols, has led the church astray by promising what the serpent promised Eve in the Garden: "You will be like God, knowing good and evil."

The ideas of ancient Greek philosophy were subordinate to the Bible until the Enlightenment, but they have since gained independence and evolved into scientific materialism (an alternate form of knowledge to the Bible) and secularism and cultural Marxism (an alternate morality from the Bible). These philosophies have worked together in tandem to provide man with the autonomy and proprietary right to define these two key issues for humanity. Like the serpent's deception in the Garden, the seduction and delusion of our culture and the church has occurred with such stealth that we are largely unaware it has even taken place. My aim in this short book is to expose these deceptive philosophies for the lies they are so we as believers can escape the discipline of delusion, resubmit ourselves to the authority of God's knowledge and morality, and abide in Christ.

In Ephesians 5:14, Paul commands the church, "Awake, sleeper, and arise from the dead, and Christ will shine on you." The church cannot shine the light of Christ on a culture which has expunged Christ from the church.

This book addresses how Christ has been evicted and how His followers can repent and once again be salt and light in a dying world. Although exploring these ideas may seem tedious, understanding them is essential to us as believers becoming aware of the insidious forces destroying our faith. My aim is to expose these ideas so we can awaken from the deception of idolatry and live as pure and obedient lights to the world.

Finally, I wish to make a note about my audience. I am a layman, and I am writing to other laymen. I am not a philosopher, historian, scientist, or theologian, nor is my focus on reaching these professionals, despite my great respect and admiration for their work. Those with such training will see me for the amateur that I am. When addressing any of the above topics, to the best of my knowledge, I am writing accurately. But I write as a layman to other laymen who seek to glorify the Lord Jesus Christ! Further, I am not writing as a Christian apologist but as a Christian. I aim to contend for the faith, not defend it against her attackers. The Lord Jesus will both build and defend His church, and in this He does not need the likes of me.

My intended audience is (though by no means exclusively) men who take seriously their responsibility for the spiritual oversight of their families. We need to understand the world around us, what produced us, how far we have deviated from the truth, and how to biblically respond to the lies. Ultimately, we must read our culture through Scripture and not the other way around. If we do this, we will likely be among only a few who both take this responsibility seriously and understand our culture. We must teach our families and whoever else will listen to recognize the idol's temple that is now in our midst.

CHAPTER 1

Purpose

IN SEVENTH GRADE, I attended a confirmation class in preparation to become a member of our church. While studying the Ten Commandments, the commandment forbidding idolatry particularly stood out to me. I remember saying to myself, *Well, at least that's one thing we don't have to worry about anymore!*

I no longer believe that.

In fact, I believe that idolatry is our chief sin and has destroyed both Judeo-Christian culture, which was produced by people who believe the Bible, and institutional Christianity. God will always have His remnant elect, but biblical Christianity is being expunged not just from the public square, but from the institutional church as well.

Philosophy Has Become the New Idolatry

While idolatry in the Old Testament constituted graven images crafted by the *hands* of men, the most subtle and destructive idols in modern times are philosophies crafted by the *minds* of men. In Colossians 2:8, Paul writes, "See to it that no one takes you captive through philosophy and empty deception, according to the tradition of men, according to the elementary principles of the world, rather than according to Christ."

In my thirty years of ministry, no one has ever said to me, "Bangert, I need help. I've been taken captive by philosophy!" Yet I contend that our culture and the church have been taken captive by philosophy without realizing it. The West is the first culture to deliberately reject Christianity and the culture it produced. This philosophical assault was deliberate and rapid, and we offered scant resistance, all too often enthusiastically embracing it. As a result, Western culture and the church are now unwittingly held captive by it.

My aim is to explain how idolatry has become philosophical in nature, and how these philosophies have captured and destroyed the heart of the culture and the church.

To understand idolatry, we must first understand the proper relationship between God and man. This relationship is based on the authority of God as Creator, and flows from God to man through two strategic modalities: knowledge and morality.

Only Scripture Can Define What Is Real

By knowledge I mean factual truth, i.e. what is real. Why do we need God to tell us what is real? Because

Scripture describes a spiritual reality that we do not ordinarily directly experience. Scripture refers to this spiritual reality as the "heavenly places" (Ephesians 1:3, 20; 2:6; 3:10; 6:12), the realm where God and His angels battle Satan and his demons, and the true home of all who belong to Christ. Ephesians 6:12 tells us, "For our struggle is not against flesh and blood, but against the rulers, against the powers, against the world forces of this darkness, against the spiritual forces of wickedness in the heavenly places." This is information we would not have known if Scripture had not told us. Scripture reveals that Jesus has gone ahead there to "prepare a place" for us with Him (John 14:3), and therefore God's people are asked to seek that "city which has foundations, whose architect and builder is God" (Hebrews 11:10).

Furthermore, this spiritual reality, anchored in the Godhead, is not just our home for the future—it superintends the natural world of the past, present, and future. By superintend, I mean that it directs, oversees, and manages the course of all earthly events, both large and small.

Many passages in Scripture draw back the veil to reveal how this underlying spiritual reality in the universe continuously impacts temporal events. The author of 2 Kings relays a particularly memorable example. In chapter six, Elisha and his servant find themselves surrounded by the powerful Aramean army. His servant responds with seemingly justifiable despair. But Elisha offers a surprising reassurance: "Do not fear, for those who are with us are more than those are with them" (verse 16). He then prays for the Lord to open the eyes of his servant. "And the Lord opened the servant's eyes and he saw; and behold, the mountain was full of horses and chariots of fire all around Elisha" (verse 17). Elisha then prays for the Arameans to be struck with blindness and leads his helpless opponents away into Samaria. This spectacular event was not just an isolated example of an Old Testament miracle no longer relevant today. First Corinthians 10:20, and even more vividly, the books of Job, Daniel and Revelation, allude to this unseen realm of spiritual forces impacting all of the events on earth.

In other words, the unseen spiritual realm is the cause of all of the events of history, for, "Who is there who speaks and it comes to pass unless the Lord has commanded it? Is it not from the mouth of the Most High that good and ill go forth?" (Lamentations 3:37–38). Things are not as they seem, and as the people of God, we must keep our eyes and hope on the reality underlying our experience.

Only Scripture Can Define What Is Good

The second way that God tethers His people to Himself is through morality, or moral truth, i.e. by defining what is good and what is evil. God alone reserves this right to define good and evil, and He communicates it to us through the biblical commandments. The biblical commandments serve as our tie to truth and our means of knowing God, who is the ultimate truth. John tells us, "He who has My commandments and keeps them, he it is who loves Me; and he who loves Me shall be loved by My Father, and I will love him, and will disclose myself to him" (John 14:21).

From the very beginning, God expected man to accept His revelation of true knowledge and morality by faith. He initially defined His morality by a single commandment—the prohibition from eating from the Tree of the Knowledge of Good and Evil. The Tree represented not the *ability to discern* right and wrong (or capacity for moral discernment) but rather the *right to define* it. If Adam and Eve had possessed no moral conscience, God could not have held them morally culpable for disobedience. But man never wanted to walk by faith; he wanted instead to determine what is true and what is right for himself. This quest for autonomy led not only to the Fall in Genesis 3, but to idolatry as the means to follow our own way. Thus, redefining knowledge and morality lies at the heart of modern idolatry/philosophy.

How can we equate philosophy with idolatry? What god is being served? The god that humanity has longed to worship from the very beginning: man! Man and his wisdom—man as the measure of all things with no accountability and no consequences—determining for himself what is in his best interest. The quest for autonomy began in the rebellion of Eden with the serpent's promise, "You will be like God" (Genesis 3:5). Thus the Tree of the Knowledge of Good and Evil was the first idol, and it became the prototype for all subsequent idolatry. This idolatry found expression again in the tower of Babel when a united humanity said, "Come let us make a name for ourselves" (Genesis 11:4), or in other words, come let us make ourselves gods. These are the purest expressions in the Bible of the kind of idolatry that now surrounds us.

But God thwarted man's desire for autonomy by confusing his language at Babel. As a result, the human race was unable to live and act as a united people. Instead, the various nations were forced into a more limited and less universal form of self-determination. The Old Testament next depicts idolatry in its most easily recognizable form, the worship of graven images. These graven images acted as surrogates for man to continue "worship[ping] and serv[ing] the creature rather than the Creator" (Romans 1:25). These idolatrous substitutes, worshipped by the nations around them, ensnared Israel for the next thousand years. The way of the nations, whose cultures were built upon the lies of idolatry, never ceased alluring the Jewish people.

Ancient Israel Worshipped God and Idols . . . and We Have Continued the Practice

Thus syncretistic worship, the blending of the worship of God with the idolatry of their neighbors, became Israel's means of maintaining both their autonomy and the illusion that they were worshipping God. Jeremiah calls this a "discipline of delusion," saying that despite "learn[ing] the way of the nations," Israel mistakenly believed that they were still serving God (Jeremiah 10:2–3, 8). Thus, they were deluded, unable to see their syncretism as idolatry. Ironically, God used those very nations, whose gods and customs Israel so loved, to ultimately destroy the nation of Israel.

However, today we no longer believe in the ancient gods. Because of this, in these latter days of the church age, we have returned to our original and most naked expression of autonomy: our desire to treat man as an end in himself rather than a means to the end of bringing glory to God. The simplicity of man-worship began to reemerge with the ancient Greeks, who built a worldview and culture on human reason alone without the aid of the gods. Plato's *Republic* offers a carefully and skillfully articulated vision in which philosopher kings rule by virtue of having the greatest and most educated intellect. Under their watchful eyes, philosopher kings arrange marriages, and the community, rather than the parents, raises the children ("it takes a village to raise a child"). Newborns deemed unfit by the rulers are abandoned to die of exposure. And all is done for the eternal glory of man.

Although this vision did not come to fruition, Greek philosophy eventually became the "way of the nations" that the early church found appealing. In the early centuries of Christianity, as the Roman Empire faltered and Christianity gained acceptance, Christian theologians, including Origen, Clement, and Augustine, incorporated some of Plato's ideas into Christian doctrine to explain the Trinity. They also employed the erudition of the Greeks to attract the more educated classes. Later, Saint Thomas Aquinas and others synthesized Aristotle's ideas into Christian thought.

We Have Made Idols of Ourselves

In synthesizing Greek philosophy to Christianity, man took the first important step towards making an idol of himself. With the synthesis, the ideas of philosophy were not only preserved but given status and esteem within Christianity. Beginning in Late Antiquity and extending well into the late Middle Ages, philosophy was considered the handmaiden of theology. But then a second and perhaps more important step was taken. The handmaiden turned on her mistress. It took several centuries, but when the handmaiden completed her mission, her mistress was dead. As with Israel, God allowed the adulteress to be destroyed by her lovers, in this case, the philosophies of men.

My aim is to trace the murder and identify the assassins.

For centuries, the church controlled the culture and drank freely from the philosophies of the past without losing its authority. Though it rarely fully obeyed the Bible, during that time the church (and the culture it produced) nevertheless recognized Scripture as the primary source of moral and factual truth. But with the advent of the Scientific Revolution and the Enlightenment, intellectuals began emancipating themselves from the authority of Christianity.

Science and secularism (seeking the purported well-being of mankind apart from religion) have worked in tandem, reinforcing and supporting one another. In science, intellectuals found a means of defining knowledge apart from the authority of the Scripture. While science did not conflict with biblical Christianity, scientism or scientific materialism did, because it offered an alternative to the biblical worldview that a spiritual reality underlies experience, claiming instead that nothing exists except for the material world, the world of matter and energy. Science's great successes bolstered the belief that modern man knows more than any who preceded us and lent credence to the newly revised morality. Finally, science aided intellectuals' belief in the myth of progress—a utopian vision whereby we gain mastery over all creation. In secular philosophy, intellectuals defined morality for themselves, a morality in which the well-being of mankind in this life is all that matters.

Though the church sought accommodation with this evolving world of enlightenment and began embracing its ideas, the secular world did not reciprocate, but rather grew increasingly hostile toward the church. As in Old

Testament Israel, where the idols of the nations were numerous and varied, the ideologies that emerged from the Enlightenment were similarly varied and heterogeneous. What they shared was the desire to produce a society independent from God, and together, they gradually eroded the authority of the church and threatened biblical faith within the church.

Cultural Marxism, popularly known as "political correctness," became the final nail in the coffin. Neither a benign nor benevolent philosophy, it was formulated with the express intent of destroying Western culture and Christianity. We will discuss this philosophy and its origins in greater detail later, but it is well summarized by Bill Lind in "The Origins of Political Correctness" published on the Accuracy in Academia website.[1] He notes that its key proponents did not believe people would embrace Marxism "until they [were] freed from Western culture, and particularly from the Christian religion." Cultural Marxism was devised to do this in part by first ridiculing and then denouncing biblical morality. Karl Marx wrote in *A Contribution to the Critique of Hegel's Philosophy of Right* in 1884, "The criticism of religion is the prerequisite of all criticism." Additional targets and casualties have included the nuclear family, masculinity, and finally reason itself. This assault has further destroyed not just the authority of the church in the culture, but also threatened the authority of Scripture within the church, a threat the church has poorly withstood.

Modern Philosophy Has Neutralized the Power of Scripture in the Church

The assault on the authority of Scripture in the church has effectively removed Christ and the gospel, with its emphasis on the eternal soul, from the church. There are at least two ways to judge if a church is apostate: 1) Is what it teaches biblically true? and 2) Are there truths in the Bible that it refuses to teach? Jesus tells us in Matthew 24:35, "Heaven and earth will pass away, but My words shall not pass away." He expects us therefore to obey His eternal words. In Luke 6:46, He asks, "Why do you call Me, 'Lord, Lord,' and do not do what I say?" Jesus makes obedience to Himself a litmus test to having a relationship with Him. "He who believes in the Son has eternal life; but he who does not obey the Son will not see life, but the wrath of God abides on him" (John 3:36).

Science, secularism, and cultural Marxism's influence has produced a church embarrassed about the Word of God and unwilling to fully obey it. Instead of following the apostles' original understanding of Christ's message, the modern church has reinterpreted the scriptures to accommodate the culture. Much of the modern church is ashamed to mention such countercultural topics as the differing roles of the sexes, disciplining wayward believers for disobedience, and extramarital sex or homosexuality being sins. Yet the Scripture unequivocally teaches these doctrines, and our shame of God's Word effectively neuters our ministry to the world.

Though this book is a critique of secular ideas, it is not a condemnation of the intellect or education. On the contrary, Christ is the embodiment of the truth, and all truth belongs to Him. As Christians, we should therefore seek rather than fear the truth. These idolatrous ideas are not isolated to our educational institutions—instead they permeate our culture. Education trains us to think and learn, skills vital to critically evaluating these ideas rather than passively accepting them. The prophet Daniel serves as an example of how to thrive in a hostile culture. Growing up in ancient Babylon, though he was immersed in the learning of the Chaldeans, "Daniel made up his mind that he would not defile himself" (Daniel 1:8). Because of this, he became a great man of God. Daniel's resolution must be our resolution. Central to this resolution is viewing our culture through the lens of the Bible, and not the other way around.

This leads us to the final question of where this leaves Christ's true followers. I am deeply skeptical that the culture can or will be retaken, and I do not advocate that we try. After all, God is superintending all of history. Everything is on schedule, God is in control, and He has not been surprised by any of man's hubristic "triumphs." Jesus tells us that His "kingdom is not of this world" (John 18:36). In fact, the elect of God have always suffered as a persecuted minority. Paul tells us, "All who desire to live godly in Christ Jesus will be persecuted" (2 Timothy 3:12).

If persecution is our lot, then let it be for the right reason. In John 8:31–32, Jesus says, "If you continue [abide] in My word, you are truly disciples of mine; and you will know the truth and the truth will make you free." The freedom of which He speaks is freedom from sin. To be free we must abide, or live with Him now. To live with Him we must return to following His Word in its totality. And to live with Him means being the enemy of the world. But like the deluded idolaters in Jeremiah 10:8, we have become friends with the world, unable to recognize our idolatry.

Most Christians I know believe we are in or near the end times. We cannot be sure if this is so. But if we are near the end times, Scripture tells us that, of necessity, we must also be in the midst of apostasy. In 2 Thessalonians 2:3, Paul links apostasy (a falling away of the church) with the return of the Lord, saying, "It will not come unless the apostasy comes first." He says of the majority, "They did not receive the love of the truth so as to be saved. For this reason God will send upon them a deluding influence so that they will believe what is false, in order that they all may be judged who did not believe the truth but took pleasure in wickedness" (2 Thessalonians 2:10b–12).

I do not know if we are living in the apostasy of the end times, but I have no doubt that we have fallen into a very deep apostasy. I plead with us as biblical Christians to repent while there is time. For whether or not His return is imminent, our time on earth will be over very soon.

We will be dead a lot longer than we will be alive, and the thesis of Scripture is that we should plan accordingly! The time is now!

But despite the dark times, we have great hope. Greater is He who is in us than he who is in the world!

CHAPTER 2

God, Knowledge, and Morality

THERE IS NO logically necessary relationship between God on the one hand and knowledge and morality on the other. For example, the ancient Greeks did not look to their gods for either knowledge or morality. One can hardly blame them for this; their gods were certainly not prime examples of moral excellence. They routinely committed adultery, murder, deception, and incest. For example, the chief of the gods, Zeus, was rescued by his mother from being eaten by his father, and went on to marry his own sister and sire children by more than 60 other women, one of whom he raped. W. J. Conybeare and J. S. Howson in their book, *The Life and Epistles of St. Paul*, note:

> It is enough to say with Seneca, that "no other effect could possibly be produced, but that all shame on account of sin must be taken away from men, if they believe in such gods;" and with Augustine, that "Plato himself, who saw well the

depravity of the Greek gods, and has seriously censured them, better deserves to be called a god than those ministers of sin."

Man's Sin Is to Define Knowledge and Morality on His Own Terms

Since the Greeks saw no reason to connect knowledge and morality to their gods, they invented philosophy. Their philosophical quest was not only intended to discover knowledge about the natural, physical world, but also to discern moral knowledge about how men ought to live their lives. The effort began in earnest with Socrates and continued with his disciples, Plato and Aristotle. The modern moral philosopher Susan Neiman observes in her book, *Moral Clarity: A Guide for Grown-up Idealists*:

> Socrates was the first to insist that we should rise above whatever particular mire happens to grip us, in order to seek something better and truer. He was thereby the first to introduce moral concepts backed by no authority but our own ability to reason.

From Socrates on, Greek philosophy grounded both knowledge and morality in human reason.

The quest to ground knowledge and morality in human reason alone was resurrected in the eighteenth century Enlightenment and forms the basis for the ideologies of our age. My contention is that this is the heart and soul of idolatry: to ground knowledge and morality in something other than the biblical God. But defining knowledge and morality is not an end in itself; rather it serves as the means to the all-consuming end of autonomy.

Man has relentlessly pursued autonomy since the Garden of Eden. His rejection of God's authority to define knowledge and morality is not only foolish and sinful, but has led to the corruption of his ability to discern moral and factual truth. Although God intervened in history, reconnecting knowledge and morality to Himself through His revelation recorded in the Old and New Testaments, unfortunately the church, like Israel, has chosen to follow the culture in their disobedience, divorcing us from the truth as well. For Israel, the pursuit of autonomy was manifested in pagan idolatry; for the modern church, in pagan philosophy.

God never intended for man to define truth for himself. From Genesis to Revelation, God insists that knowledge and morality originate with Him and Him alone. In fact, the authority of God to do so is the premise of the scriptures, which insist that the root of all man's problems is his persistent unwillingness to submit to that authority. The book of Isaiah begins with this indictment: "Sons I have reared and brought up, but they have revolted against Me" (Isaiah 1:2).

We see this in the first three chapters of the book of Genesis, which demonstrate that God is the sovereign Creator of all things and that everything He created is good. For this reason, in the Garden of Eden God claims the moral and sovereign prerogative to link knowledge and morality to each other and to Himself in the Tree of the Knowledge of Good and Evil. God's message to them and to us in so doing is essentially this: "Do you want a relationship with Me? Then you have to abstain from the Tree of the Knowledge of Good and Evil—that is, whatever you know and how you behave must emanate from Me. We're a unity. I'm going to define knowledge for you, and I'm going to define morality for you." His authority to define these is predicated on the fact that only He understands the true basis of reality and what is good.

If Adam and Eve had obeyed and agreed to walk by faith in His revelation of what was true and what was good, their relationship with Him would have remained intact. But in their quest for autonomy, they defied God, and in so doing, chose to define knowledge and morality for themselves. Sin broke the unity between God, knowledge, and morality. This quest for autonomy continued to be the primordial impulse in all their children, expressed in various forms of idolatry.

Knowledge and Morality Create a Worldview That Directs Our Lives

Why are knowledge and morality so important, and

how do they function in our lives? Knowledge of what reality is and the morality that flows from it answer the fundamental metaphysical questions of life and form the basis of our worldview. Our worldview in turn determines and motivates our behavior, informing the way we live.

Some of the most important metaphysical questions are: What is the ultimate nature of reality, material or spiritual? Is nature governed by deterministic materialistic laws, or does the spiritual superintend, or govern, the natural? How does the universe work, how did it begin, and how will it end? Do humans have souls and, if so, what is the fate of the soul? Is man the product of blind, random processes, or is there a purpose for our existence, and if so, what is it? Is there a God, what is He like, and does He have expectations of humans? Is man accountable, and if so, on what basis and by what sort of God will he be judged? Or is truth relative and man autonomous? Is man a sinner capable of moral choice or a blank slate molded and victimized by his environment? What is our relationship to the earth, plants and animals? What happens to us after we die?

All these questions are answered by a person's worldview—what he believes about knowledge and morality—and will alter the way a man lives. For example, Hindus believe that their present circumstances result from their behavior in a past life. Therefore, those with a Hindu worldview are not encouraged to help their neighbors because doing so interferes with their karma. In the Christian worldview, however, charity is considered a virtue because we are commanded by Christ to love our neighbors as Christ has loved us in dying for us (1 John 4:11). In Christianity, there is no past life, but "it is appointed for men to die once and after this comes judgment" (Hebrews 9:27). Both an individual Hindu and Christian may exhibit charity; but only Christianity incorporates charity into its worldview.

All of these important questions about the true nature of reality must be answered by faith for the theist and atheist alike, for we have no direct proof regardless of our belief system. The various religions answer these questions in their own unique ways, and modern science answers them in another way, but all answer by faith. No matter who we are, we all have presuppositions that we are forced to base our lives on but cannot prove. It is as though God has woven faith into the fabric of the universe. The unavoidability of death forces us each to make a choice what to believe. There is no escape: everybody must have faith. The thesis of the Scripture is, chose wisely in what you place your faith.

God Is a Superior Source of Knowledge and Morality Because He Stands Outside of Time and Space

What makes God a better choice than man as a source for knowledge and morality? Because He is God and we are not, God's knowledge is infinite and ours finite. Our intellect is simply insufficient for the task of comprehending all of reality.

Science tells us that our galaxy, the Milky Way, is 100,000 light years in diameter and home to roughly 100 billion stars. And there are at least 200 billion other galaxies in the universe, also containing 100 billion stars or more. How much do we know about most of those galaxies and stars and their accompanying solar systems?

Yet scientists believe that this vast expanse of space makes up less than five percent of the material universe. The remainder of the universe is composed of dark matter, which comprises 27 percent and about which we know almost nothing, and dark energy, which composes 68 percent and about which we know even less. Although scientists believe that these two entities exist based on the calculations of physics, we currently have no direct means of seeing, feeling, touching, measuring, or studying them. Science may one day understand more about these two entities; but today we understand only a miniscule portion of the material world.

But the Bible teaches that our ignorance is infinitely more profound than this. Hebrews 11:1 tells us, "Now faith is the assurance of things hoped for, the conviction of things not seen." God asks us to walk by faith in these two key areas we cannot appreciate on our own: the unseen and the future.

We will begin with the future. Our lives are complex,

with a nearly infinite number of variables impinging on us at any given moment. Not only do we not know what will happen to us tomorrow or in ten years, but we do not know the unintended consequences of the choices we are in control of making today.

Let's compare our lives to the game of checkers, a seemingly simple game involving only two players. In an article published in the prestigious journal *Science* in 2007, scientists triumphantly proclaimed, "Checkers is solved." This enormous project required a team of PhDs running 50 computers nearly continuously for 18 years. Their efforts determined that there were an overwhelming 500 billion billion (5×10^{20}) possible positions for all of the pieces on the board!

As a gross underestimate, let us assume that our lives are 100 times more complicated than the game of checkers. Let's also assume that a game of checkers takes one hour to play, and that we will each live eighty years, or approximately 700,000 hours. That would mean that there are roughly 350 billion billion billion (35×10^{28}) different bits of information necessary to run our lives. But as staggering as that is, it is not the most important point. The critical point is that the only reason checkers could be solved in the first place is because a human being designed the game and wrote the rules. That is, we know all the rules of checkers because we wrote them. We, on the other hand, did not design the universe or write the rules of life, and we have no tools at our disposal to discover the rulebook on our own. And no matter what we do, we have no means to look beyond the grave.

But God in Exodus 3:14 (and later Jesus in John 8:58) calls Himself the great "I AM," thus claiming existence outside of time, and therefore a perfect understanding of the past, present, and future. And as Creator, He designed the universe and wrote its rules. Because this is so, His ability to outthink us in terms of what is right and good exceeds ours to a degree that is not even worthy of comparison.

God stands not only outside of time, but outside of space as well. He exists in the unseen spiritual world which we do not directly experience. The Bible not only says that we are out of touch with reality, but that this reality to which we are blind is the true cause of all things. The spiritual is the realm of causes, and the temporal/earthly is the realm of effects. As we noted in the previous chapter, in Lamentations 3:37–38, Jeremiah states, "Who is there who speaks and it comes to pass, unless the Lord has commanded it? Is it not from the mouth of the Most High that good and ill go forth?" We experience good and ill; we do not experience God commanding it. Isaiah 45:46–47 teaches this same truth: "That men may know from the rising to the setting of the sun that there is no one besides me. I am the LORD and there is no other. The One forming light and creating darkness, causing well-being and creating calamity; I am the LORD who does all these."

Although we may experience ill from the hand of God, the issue is intent. The intent of God is always our good, and this overrides every other force, including the evil intentions of men. In Genesis 50:20, Joseph says to his brothers who sold him into slavery, "You meant evil against me, but God meant it for good in order to bring about this present result, to preserve many people alive." Scripture reminds us of the purpose of both the good and ill we experience in Hebrews 12:10–11: "That we may share His holiness," and that "afterwards [this discipline] yields the peaceful fruit of righteousness."

The book of Revelation also delineates the sovereignty of God. In chapter 5, God the Father holds a scroll with seven seals. One by one, Christ opens these seals, each unleashing a calamity on earth, which is mediated by an angel. I suggest that this is not unique to Revelation but is rather the blueprint for all that happens on earth. Not every event proceeds from a broken seal and angelic intervention, but every event does result from a spiritual action. We see from this the formula for the operation of the universe: spiritual cause→temporal effect.

In this way, we are intertwined with the spiritual. But Scripture makes an additional point: our earthly actions have spiritual (and therefore eternal) consequences. The Fall in the Garden illustrates this truth. In Romans 8:19–22, Paul teaches that the whole of creation was corrupted by man's sin in the Garden. But Hebrews 9:11–12, 23 illustrates that not only was earth corrupted by our sin on earth, but also heaven:

> But when Christ appeared as a high priest of the good things to come, He entered through the greater and more perfect tabernacle, not made with hands, that is to say, not of this creation; and not through the blood of goats and calves, but through His own blood, He entered the holy place once for all, having obtained eternal redemption.... Therefore it was necessary for the copies of the things in heaven [i.e. the earthly tabernacle] to be cleansed with [the blood of bulls and goats], but the heavenly things themselves with better sacrifices than these [i.e. the blood of Christ].

Through this, we learn the astonishing truth that the heavenly tabernacle was polluted by sin committed on earth and needed to be cleansed by the blood of Christ.

The point is this: the spiritual and temporal worlds are a two-way street. Jesus Christ is sovereign over earth, but what we do on earth has profound spiritual implications for each of us that will last for eternity. As citizens of heaven, we must live with the spiritual reality of the universe in mind. We are commanded to "work out [our] salvation with fear and trembling" while on earth (Philippians 2:12) because doing so shapes the quality of our eternities (1 Corinthians 3:10–15). For this reason, in Ephesians 6:12, Paul reminds us to focus on this action in the spiritual realm, "For our struggle is not against flesh and blood, but against the rulers, against the powers, against the world forces of darkness, against the spiritual forces of wickedness in the heavenly places."

Since the spiritual realm is the realm of causes, and the physical realm is the realm of effects, it is this spiritual dimension of life to which the people of God must remain tethered. Biblical morality does this for us, and God in turn reveals true knowledge to His followers. This is important in understanding not just the Fall but also the current state of the church.

Knowledge and Morality Apart from God Is Stupid and Sinful

But Adam, in acting upon his desire for autonomy, cut the tether between morality and God, defying God and becoming the first human sinner. However, I suggest that before Adam became a sinner, he was stupid. The notion that man not only is smart enough and moral enough to run his own life, but that he can oppose God and win, is the height of stupidity. In his stupidity, he listened to the two related evil ideas planted by Satan with the temptation.

The first is embedded in the serpent's question in 3:1: "Indeed, has God said, 'You shall not eat from any tree of the garden'?" The question both impugned the veracity of God and subtly questioned His goodness, despite all God's good provision for them. With a single lie, Satan challenged what God had spoken and depicted Him as withholding something good from them. He thereby covertly called into question God's right to define knowledge and morality—why in fact should He if He is not truthful or good?

The second idea is found in verse 5: "For God knows that in the day you eat from it your eyes will be opened, and you will be like God, knowing good and evil." With it, Satan implied that man could therefore replace God and define morality and knowledge for himself.

On these two ideas—1) God isn't good/doesn't have your best interest at heart, and 2) You can replace Him—are built the modern ideologies that have crippled the church today. These two ideas form a fault line through the human soul, and our modern philosophies were designed to fill that fault line. No matter how complex and sophisticated these ideologies may appear, this is their foundation.

In other words, ideas were at the heart of the temptation, ideas that struck a resonant chord with our lust for autonomy. This is the first recorded instance in the Bible of ideas being deployed for nefarious purposes, but it will not be the last. Note also that the ideas contained a subtle blend of truth and lies, both causing confusion and making the lies more palatable. Satan has continued to recycle this strategy as he seeks to turn men away from God in our time, and man has continued to believe his lies because they justify his quest for autonomy.

Therefore, God can justly charge humanity with two crimes: 1) sin, "for all have sinned and fall short of the glory of God" (Romans 3:23), and 2) stupidity, for "all mankind is stupid, devoid of knowledge" (Jeremiah 10:14; 51:17). Sin and stupidity are traveling companions. Paul tells us that we are neither righteous nor do we understand (Romans 3:10–11). By listening to the serpent rather than God, we have become stupid sinners, practicing a corrupted morality and deluded by a distorted understanding of reality.

Jesus Christ Is the Embodiment of God's Knowledge and Morality

But in the Mosaic Law, we begin to see God reestablishing knowledge and morality as having their origin from Him, a reunion that is ultimately completed in Christ. He begins by defining morality for His people. In the Old Testament, it is defined by the Mosaic Law, and in the New Testament by the commandments of Jesus and the apostles.

Moses commands Israel in Deuteronomy 4:6, "So keep and do [God's laws], for that is your wisdom and your understanding in the sight of the peoples who will hear all these statutes and say, 'Surely this great nation is a wise and understanding people.'" Moses' words reveal that in man's redemption, morality must precede knowledge. In other words, we cannot accurately understand the truth unless we are willing to accept God's morality. This idea that one cannot have true knowledge of reality apart from accepting God's morality is not intuitive; but it is one of the foundational principles of Scripture.

This concept that submission to God's morality is necessary for understanding truth is confirmed in the New Testament. Jesus Himself echoes this doctrine in John 7:17: "If anyone is willing to do His will, he will know of the teaching, whether it is of God or whether I speak from Myself." In other words, obedience (accepting God's morality) is essential for recognizing the truth (knowledge). He tells us in John 14:6: "I am the way and the truth and the life; no one comes to the Father but through Me." One cannot arrive at truth without Jesus Christ because He is the truth.

So to whom does he reveal His truth? Jesus declares in John 14:21, "He who has My commandments and keeps them is the one who loves Me; and he who loves Me will be loved by my Father, and I will love him and will disclose Myself to him." The One who is the embodiment of truth, "in whom are hidden all the treasures of wisdom and knowledge" (Colossians 2:3), will disclose Himself only to the obedient. Thus obedience to God's commandments is requisite for understanding truth. As His Father did in the Old Testament, so Jesus in the New Testament weds morality and knowledge to Himself and maintains that apart from Him, our ability to discern moral and factual truth is compromised.

The Sole Purpose of Human Reason Is to Know God

In Romans 1, the apostle Paul provides a blueprint of how man's great divorce from God's truth has tragically unfolded for humanity. The passage delineates the destruction of the ability to discern true knowledge that has resulted from denying God's morality in the three progressive "God gave them over" statements.

Because man has turned from God to sin, God has delivered him over to that sin. First, in verse 24, he says, "Therefore God gave them over in the lusts of their hearts to impurity, so that their bodies would be dishonored among them." In this we see Him giving them over to heterosexual immorality in disobedience to God. Second, in verses 26–27, He gives them over to immorality, this time of a homosexual nature: "For this reason God gave them over to degrading passions; for their women exchanged the natural function for that which is unnatural, and in the same way also the men abandoned the natural function of the woman and burned in their desire toward one another, men with men committing indecent acts and receiving in their own persons the due penalty of their error." Finally, in verse 28, we see the finale: "And just as they did not see fit to acknowledge God any longer, God gave them over to a depraved mind, to do those things which are not proper." Paul is saying that the immorality of the preceding verses causes God to give them a depraved mind, by which they are now shut off from truth, knowledge and reality.

Because they are guilty of "suppress[ing] the truth in unrighteousness" (v. 18), God delivers them over to their own lies. Their immorality severs the thin tether to the reality of the spiritual (truth), so that, "Professing to be wise, they became fools, and exchanged the glory of the incorruptible God for an image in the form of corruptible man and of birds and four footed animals and crawling creatures" (Romans 1:22–23).

God gave us reason for one purpose only: to know Him (Jeremiah 9:23–24; 1 Corinthians 10:31; Colossians 3:17, 23). Paul's point is not that men who deny God can no longer think, but rather that they lose the ability to use their minds for the singular purpose for which God gave it. This closes men off from God's eternal truth and goodness. Romans 1 is a startlingly accurate description of the moral degeneration our current culture has taken in just two generations, and the modern church is rapidly following suit.

To summarize, God and God alone must define morality and knowledge for mankind. This truth forms the backbone of the scriptures. In our quest for autonomy, the people of God in the Old Testament, New Testament and today rebel against this and seek to establish our own authority and identity in such matters. I suggest that this is the heartbeat of man and the heartbeat of idolatry. It is as pernicious and destructive today as any Old Testament or pagan idolatry. But it comes in a different form from the worship of graven images; it comes in the form of ideas, which is the subject of the next chapter.

CHAPTER 3

The Discipline of Delusion

IN THE LAST chapter, we established that God must be the source of morality and knowledge for His people. In this chapter, we will explore how to avoid idolatry—He must be the only source. That is, the entirety of our worldview must derive solely from God and what He reveals about knowledge and morality in His Word.

Our Relationship with Jesus Is Binary

In His warning to the church of Laodicea in Revelation 3:14–22, Jesus highlights several important features of their walk with God. He castigates them, saying, "I know your deeds, that you are neither cold nor hot; I wish that you were cold or hot. So because you are lukewarm, and neither hot nor cold, I will spit you out of My mouth" (verses 15–16).

The first point to note is that our relationship with Jesus is binary. He tells us in Matthew 12:30 that our relationship with Him is an all-or-nothing proposition:

"He who is not with Me is against Me; and he who does not gather with Me scatters." Even before the computer was invented, Jesus tells us that He, His truth, and life itself are written in binary code. Contrary to our perception of reality, there are only two paths in life, the path through the narrow gate and that through the wide gate (Matthew 7:13–14). Lukewarm deeds result from attempting to harmonize the wisdom and morality of the world (cold) with the wisdom and morality of God (hot).

But Jesus tells us that the two are incompatible. In reality, a man can be either hot or cold, a one or a zero. But men believe that with God there can be fractions, and Jesus advises us in these two short verses in Revelation that God will not tolerate such ambivalence. We can be either hot or cold, and trying to live a lukewarm life is the mistake of our lives. I contend that the modern church has become lukewarm by the syncretism of ideas, mixing the wisdom of the world with the Bible.

He goes on to tell them, "You say, 'I am rich, and have become wealthy, and have need of nothing,' and you do not know that you wretched and miserable and poor and blind and naked" (verse 17). In this statement, we see the second truth, that lukewarmness is a delusional state. The Laodiceans could not be more mistaken about the health of their relationship with Christ. They believe they are rich, when in fact He says they are poor. Unawareness, not understanding the condition of their relationship with Christ, is symptomatic of those who compromise with the world. Israel fell into syncretistic idolatry and became deluded, and the church is repeating their mistake.

The purpose of this chapter is to examine Israel's syncretism and the delusion that resulted from it in order to better understand our own.

Idolatry Prevents Us from Looking to God as Our Source of Knowledge and Morality

God intended to be the only source of knowledge and morality for His people; idolatry thwarts this transfer from God to His followers. Jeremiah characterizes Israel's idolatry as a "discipline of delusion" (Jeremiah 10:8), and in order to first understand their idolatry, and subsequently our own, we must understand the source and the two salient features of idolatry, which are captured by these two words, *discipline* and *delusion*.

Chapter 10 of Jeremiah is a polemic against idolatry. In verses two and three he warns:

> Do not learn the way of the nations, and do not be terrified by the signs of the heavens although the nations are terrified by them; for the customs of the peoples are delusion; because it is wood cut from the forest, the work of the hands of a craftsman with a cutting tool.

The nations' "way" refers to their conduct while on the road of life, while their "customs" refer to the ordinances or statutes that define this conduct. Taken together, they create a culture with an underlying worldview that Israel was forbidden to learn or emulate.

Whenever Israel violated this warning, it succumbed to idolatry. This is hardly surprising since idolatry contributed the intellectual framework for the way and customs of the nations. The idols gave them knowledge, but knowledge that contradicted the truths of God. Therefore, God commanded Israel to shun the nations' way and customs along with their associated idolatrous worldview.

But we are not accustomed to thinking of idolatry as "intellectual," so how can a worldview be idolatrous? Jeremiah 10:8 clarifies: "But they are altogether stupid and foolish in their discipline of delusion—their idol is wood!" The Hebrew word translated "discipline" refers to a mode of instruction. The same word appears four times in the first eight verses of Proverbs but is translated "instruction":

> To know wisdom and *instruction*, to discern the sayings of understanding, to receive *instruction* in wise behavior, righteousness, justice and equity … The fear of the LORD is the beginning of knowledge; fools despise wisdom and *instruction*. Hear, my son, your father's *instruction*, and do not forsake your mother's teaching" (verses 2, 3, 7, 8, italics added).

Today we use the word *discipline* in much the same way when we refer to the disciplines of economics, chemistry, medicine, and other academic fields. A discipline provides a means of ordering and understanding the world, and in Old Testament Israel, God's people were commanded to learn that only from Him and not from the idols. The idolatrous worldview learned from the nations, with its accompanying immorality, forms the "discipline" half of the equation.

Delusion characterizes two aspects of discipline (or instruction), its content, and the state of its students. The Hebrew word for "delusion" in Jeremiah 10:8 is *hebel*, the same word Solomon uses extensively in Ecclesiastes, which is translated "vanity" or "emptiness." "'Vanity (*hebel*) of vanities (*hebel*)' says the Preacher, 'Vanity (*hebel*) of vanities (*hebel*)! All is vanity (*hebel*)" (Ecclesiastes 1:2). This is no coincidence, since the ruler of this world offers only empty promises, whether those promises emanate from a graven idol as in Old Testament Israel, or the mouths of unregenerate men in our day. Unlike God, he is not the sovereign of history and can only offer lies and unfulfilled promises to those who follow him, for "he is a liar and the father of lies" (John 8:44).

Idolaters Aren't Aware That They're Idolaters

This brings us to the second aspect of delusion, namely that its practitioner is not aware he is an idolater. A delusion is different from an illusion. In both cases, the senses are deceived. In the case of an illusion, the one experiencing the illusion knows that his senses are deceived and that he is not experiencing reality. A shimmering hot street in the summertime is a good example. Though we perceive water in the distance, experience has taught us that this is merely an optical illusion and what our eyes perceive is not real. The eye is deceived but the mind is not.

A delusion differs because the mind is deceived: the one suffering from it is unaware that he is not experiencing reality. In psychiatry, someone suffering from schizophrenia hears voices that are not there, but in his delusion he cannot discern this. As a dermatologist, I occasionally saw patients who complained of bugs crawling on their skin. They invariably brought a baggie full of these "bugs." But the contents of the baggies revealed only bits of skin and other particles. The patients were deluded. Antimite treatment was ineffective, but an antipsychotic drug usually cured the condition.

Jeremiah is saying that, in a similar fashion, the idolater is unaware that he is practicing idolatry. This characterizes the state of the church of Laodicea, and we will see other illustrations of this shortly.

To summarize to this point:

1. God warned Israel not to learn the way and customs of the nations, which were informed by idolatry and together formed a false discipline or worldview.

2. This delusional and idolatrous worldview was vain
    or empty because it was grounded in lies about the
    nature of the world and one's conduct in it. It could
    not deliver on its promises because it emanated
    from the wrong source, for God, and not the idol,
    is sovereign.

3. It was also delusional in another sinister way in that
    the idolatrous practitioner was unaware that he was
    an idolater.

It is critical to understand that Israel's idolatry was
additive, not substitutional. In other words, it didn't *replace*
Israel's worship of God, it only *added* to it. This is what
theologians mean by syncretism. They did not abandon
the worship of the LORD but instead incorporated the
worship of other gods into their worship of Him.

We see this clearly in the worship of the golden calf
in Exodus 32:1–5:

> Now when the people saw that Moses delayed
> to come down from the mountain, the people
> assembled about Aaron, and said to him, "Come,
> make us a god who will go before us; as for this
> Moses, the man who brought us up from the
> land of Egypt, we do not know what has become
> of him." And Aaron said to them, "Tear off the
> gold rings which are in the ears of your wives,

your sons, and your daughters, and bring them to me." Then all the people tore off the gold rings which were in their ears, and brought them to Aaron. And he took this from their hand, and fashioned it with the graving tool, and made it into a molten calf; and they said, "This is your god, O Israel, who brought you up from the land of Egypt." Now when Aaron saw this, he built an altar before it; and Aaron made a proclamation and said, "Tomorrow shall be a feast to the LORD."

The punch line is in the last verse: they actually thought that they were worshipping the LORD, Jehovah, in making the golden calf. Their idolatry was syncretistic, combining the worship of God with the worship of an idol.

This passage also demonstrates how this syncretism creates a delusion. We view the event with incredulity. Making the golden calf is such obvious idolatry to us. How could they have missed it? But what is obvious to us wasn't to them. What makes this practice even more stunning is that just before this incident, the whole nation stood at the foot of a burning Mt. Sinai and heard the voice of God thundering and shaking the mountain. They all agreed it was the voice of God and trembled as He pronounced the Ten Commandments, including the second prohibiting graven images (Exodus 20:4).

So why wasn't it obvious to them? Although the text does not tell us, we do know that in pagan times, the gods and goddesses were for the most part perceived to be local deities. Each locale had its own gods, and people served those gods along with the supreme god or gods. This commonly held belief in Egypt and Canaan may have made it natural for Israel to combine their worship of Jehovah with the worship of the gods of their new home. Based on the worldview of their culture, they couldn't understand why they couldn't worship both. This illustrates the power of the delusion created by fusing the world's ideas with God's—a delusion so effective it could mute the audible commandment of God.

From that point on, this syncretistic idolatry persisted in Israel. In 1 Kings 18:21, Israel's idolatry forces Elijah into a stand-off with the prophets of Baal. "Elijah came near to all the people and said, 'How long will you hesitate between two opinions? If the LORD is God, follow Him; but if Baal, follow him.' But the people did not answer him a word." The tenacity with which Israel held to their syncretistic worship, the worship of God concurrent with the worship of Baal, is remarkable and serves as a warning to us.

Idolatry Isn't Confined to Graven Images

By the time of the Babylonian captivity, Israel's idolatry was undergoing a transformation. They began disposing of their external graven images in favor of the immaterial idols found only in the heart and mind. Consider Ezekiel 14:1–6:

> Then some elders of Israel came to me and sat down before me. And the word of the LORD came to me, saying, "Son of man, these men have set up their idols in their hearts, and have put right before their faces the stumbling block of their iniquity. Should I be consulted by them at all? Therefore speak to them and tell them, "Thus says the Lord GOD, 'Any man of the house of Israel who sets up his idols in his heart, puts right before his face the stumbling block of his iniquity, and then comes to the prophet, I the LORD will be brought to give him an answer in the matter in view of the multitude of his idols, in order to lay hold of the hearts of the house of Israel who are estranged from me through all their idols." 'Therefore say to the house of Israel, 'Thus says the Lord GOD, 'Repent and turn away from your idols and turn your faces away from all your abominations.'"

Regardless of the form, idolatry originates in the heart. In Ezekiel, God castigates Israel for idolatry even though they had dispensed with its external manifestations.

Following the Babylonian captivity, Israel continued to shun external idolatry. The leaders of the nation recognized the crucial role that idolatry had played in bringing about God's judgment and established the synagogue system to teach the people, among other things, the perils of idolatry.

Even Our Ideas Can Be Idols

This effort on their part proved highly successful to the extent that when Jesus conducted His earthly ministry in Israel, He made no mention of worshipping graven images, nor did He directly charge Israel with idolatry. But although Jesus never overtly charged them with idolatry, He did condemn them for honoring two things instead of God, implying they were guilty of idolatry of the heart.

The first is the idolatry of greed or covetousness, which Paul specifically calls idolatry in both Ephesians 5:5 and Colossians 3:5. Luke 16:14 identifies the Pharisees as lovers of money, and Jesus is repeatedly critical of this. In Matthew 6:24, He warns, "No one can serve two masters; for either he will hate the one and love the other, or he will be bold to one and despise the other. You cannot serve God and mammon." In this, we see a reiteration of the fact that our response to Jesus must be binary—either He is master, or the idol, but both cannot be. Here we see the first type of idolatry of the heart, covetousness, greed and love of money, which are identified as sin in the remainder of New Testament as well. Though this is an extremely important and prevalent idol, it is not this first idol of the heart that I now want to consider but rather a second form, the idolatry of our own ideas.

Jesus discusses this idolatry of ideology in Mark 7:6–9, when He excoriates the Pharisees for mingling their traditions with God's commands.

> And He said to them, "Rightly did Isaiah prophesy of you hypocrites, as it is written, 'This people honors me with their lips, but their heart is far away from Me. But in vain do they worship Me, teaching as doctrines the precepts of men.' Neglecting the commandments of God, you hold to the tradition of men." He was also saying to them, "You nicely set aside the commandment of God in order to keep your tradition."

In Mark 7:10–13, He elaborates,

> For Moses said, "Honor your father and your mother and, He who speaks evil of father or mother, let him be put to death;" but you say, "If a man says to his father or his mother, anything of mine you might have been helped by is Corban (that is to say, given to God)," you no longer permit him to do anything for his father or his mother; thus invalidating the word of God by your tradition which you have handed down; and you do many things such as that.

Jesus' indictment alludes to the parameters that Moses gave Israel before they entered the Promised Land: "You shall not add to the word which I am commanding you, nor take away from it, that you may keep the commandments of the LORD your God which I command you" (Deuteronomy 4:2). Note the clarity of this exhortation. God does not want His commandments tampered with, either by adding to them or by subtracting from them.

By adding their own ideas (their traditions) to God's commandments, the Pharisees ignored God's ideas (His commandments). We note from this exchange three important truths about our relationship to the commandments of God: 1) Adding our ideas to the commandments of God is sin because it usurps His role; 2) Adding to His commandments invariably leads to subtracting from them; and 3) Both of these practices are disobedience and invalidate our worship of God from His perspective.

How is this so? What is the link between worship and keeping God's commandments? Let us remember that to have a biblically true relationship with God one must allow Him to define two key issues, morality and knowledge. As we have already established, the commandments define morality, and obedience to that morality in turn reveals true knowledge.

But Jesus goes further by also linking morality to worship. What does worship of God look like, how can we know, and who will tell us? Again, the answer is that God must tell us, and He says that, at least in part, worship means keeping His commandments without modification! Samuel explains this to Saul when he disobeyed God and kept a portion of the spoil after his conquest of the Amalekites instead of destroying it entirely as God had commanded him:

> Has the LORD as much delight in burnt offerings and sacrifices as in obeying the voice of the LORD? Behold, to obey is better than sacrifice, and to heed than the fat of rams. For rebellion is as the sin of divination, and insubordination is as iniquity and idolatry (1 Samuel 15:22–23).

Whatever else we might define as worship, if we are not following the unmodified commandments of God, Jesus says it is not true worship. To summarize, the Pharisees, by adding their traditions to God's commandments, neglected the actual commandments of God, and in so doing, worshipped "in vain" according to Jesus. They were idolaters, no longer obeying and worshipping God as He actually is but obeying and worshipping God as they wished Him to be. Theirs was a syncretism of God, not with Baal, but with their own ideas.

Paul takes this teaching of Jesus with respect to Pharisaical Judaism and gives it new application to Greek and Roman philosophy. In Colossians 2:8, he warns, "See to it that no one takes you captive through philosophy and empty deception, according to the tradition of men, according to the elementary principles of the world, rather than according to Christ." In Colossians, the tradition of men of which Paul speaks refers to philosophical ideas derived from Greek and Roman philosophers. We will return to this later, but for now it is enough to understand that the traditions of a different set of men from the Pharisees, the secular philosophers, are capable of leading Christ's followers astray.

Idolatry Leads Us into Danger

As we discussed in the last chapter, the purpose of any religion or philosophy is to produce a worldview founded on principles of truth and morality by which a person can safely navigate the complexity of life. Let's turn again to Old Testament Israel to explore this.

The Law and the Prophets produced a worldview for its followers, seen in God's love and provision for Israel, His establishment of them as a nation, His production of their culture by the Mosaic Law, and His sovereignty in doing so. In addition, God continued to express His will through the prophets in those areas not specifically addressed by the Law or the culture produced by the Law.

Unfortunately, both true and false prophets arose in Israel, and the books of Isaiah and Jeremiah illustrate well the difficult tangle of truth and lies produced by the counsel of these true and false prophets. In Isaiah 3:12,

God warns wayward Jerusalem of the false prophets, "O My people! Those who guide you lead you astray, and confuse the direction of your paths." But the true prophets of God were Israel's eyes and head, sent to chart Israel's course for them by speaking for Him.

We see an example of the conflict between the true and false prophets in Jeremiah's counsel to idolatrous Israel prior to the Babylonian captivity. Consider the words of Jeremiah 21:8–10:

> You shall also say to this people, "Thus says the LORD, 'Behold, I will set before you the way of life and the way of death. He who dwells in the city will die by the sword and by famine and by pestilence; but he who goes out and falls away to the Chaldeans who are besieging you will live, and he will have his own life as booty. For I have set my face against this city for harm and not for good,' declares the LORD. 'It will be given into the hand of the king of Babylon and he will burn it with fire.'"

Jeremiah, speaking for God, instructs Israel not to resist the Babylonians or to expect victory over them but to surrender and be taken into captivity.

But many false prophets rejected Jeremiah's message and instructed Israel to choose another path. We see this in Jeremiah 28:10–11:

Then Hananiah the prophet took the yoke from the neck of Jeremiah the prophet and broke it. And Hananiah spoke in the presence of all the people, saying, "Thus says the LORD, even so will I break within two full years, the yoke of Nebuchadnezzar king of Babylon from the neck of all the nations."

God responds to this by telling Jeremiah to prophesy against Hananiah in verses 15–17:

Then Jeremiah the prophet said to Hananiah the prophet, "Listen now, Hananiah, the LORD has not sent you, and you have made this people trust in a lie. Therefore, thus says the LORD, 'Behold, I am about to remove you from the face of the earth. This year you are going to die, because you have counseled rebellion against the LORD.'" So Hananiah the prophet died in the same year in the seventh month.

From the outcome, we see that Jeremiah's counsel was proved right and Hananiah's wrong. Hananiah died, and the children of Israel were taken into captivity by Babylon. But before these events took place, the people were forced to choose whom to trust.

Citing these sections of Scripture demonstrates that the prophets, both true and false, were a source of knowledge for Israel, and that this knowledge was essential to their survival. Isaiah prophesied in 5:13, "Therefore My people go into exile for their lack of knowledge."

But how could the people know which counsel to follow? In the conflict between Jeremiah and Hananiah, this task was especially difficult because Jeremiah's counsel was not affirmed by either their reason or their desires. Reason suggests that if God was Israel's protector, He would not have allowed His people to be taken captive by a pagan empire. In addition, Jeremiah counseled abdication if not treason. Finally, Hananiah told the people what they wanted to hear, allowing them to continue in their idolatry unchecked. If you lived in Israel at the time, how would you know which prophet to follow? God intended them (and calls us) to follow the prophet who also preached repentance, in this case Jeremiah.

Idolatry Prevents Us from Seeing Our Sin

If we do not accept God's morality and fall under the influence of the idol, we become deluded and do not see our sin as sin. How can we repent of what we do not identify as sin? At this point something terrible and calamitous happens—God assists the idolater in his delusion. In Isaiah 29:10, God declares that He has done this for Israel: "For the LORD has poured over you a spirit of deep sleep, He has shut your eyes, the prophets; He has covered your heads, the seers." He says again in 6:10,

"Render the hearts of this people insensitive, their ears dull, and their eyes dim, lest they see with their eyes, hear with their ears, understand with their hearts, and return and be healed."

The Bible teaches that the inevitable consequence of this rebellion will also happen to the church before the Lord's return. In 2 Thessalonians 2:3,10–12, Paul speaks of the "man of lawlessness" who will come "with all the deception of wickedness for those who perish, because they did not receive the love of the truth so as to be saved. And for this reason God will send upon them a deluding influence so that they will believe what is false, in order that they all may be judged who did not believe the truth, but took pleasure in wickedness." Just as God assisted idolatrous Israel to believe a lie, so He also assists the idolatrous church to believe a lie. In this we see not only the effect of delusion but once again the essential linkage between God, morality and knowledge, the final dissociation of which will be the ultimate demise of humanity.

The inward movement from the idolatry of external graven images to the internal idolatry of the heart should neither trouble nor surprise us for it parallels the trajectory from Judaism to Christianity, from emphasis on external rituals and ceremonies to the inner man. For the Deceiver is not an original thinker but rather a counterfeit imitator of God. Prominent in Old Testament Judaism were the external ceremonies, rituals and sacrifices, which Satan imitated in the idolatrous practices of Israel's neighbors, always accompanied by gross immorality.

Christianity, with its core belief of being rightly related to Christ, focuses on the inner man, transformation by the renewing of the mind, and on the doctrine that is intended to transform it. Ideas and thinking are therefore central to it. Satan imitates these ideas and ideologies, which lead men away from Christ by influencing how they think. To be sure, the Old Testament anticipates this movement, but it does not find full expression until Christ.

Whatever the form of idolatry, God calls His followers to shun it and allow Him alone to define truth and goodness. A failure to recognize that God's truth is binary and cannot remain true if it is mixed with lies creates deception. And our deception will lead to judgment just as surely as it did for Israel.

Next we shall begin to examine the origins and forms of these ideas and ideologies that are deceiving the church, along with their disastrous consequences.

CHAPTER 4

The Church and Ideology

THE CHURCH HAS not only failed to escape Israel's syncretistic idolatry, but it has replicated it in every way. As we established in the last chapter, the worship of God means that He must be the sole source of knowledge and morality for His people. His truth is binary and cannot be safely combined with another truth system. This means that our worship is invalid unless we offer it on His terms, not ours. His terms dictate that we obey all of His New Testament commandments without addition, subtraction or modification.

But like Israel, we have disobeyed this command and become victims of the discipline of delusion. Mimicking them, we have not abandoned the worship of God, but combined it with the "way" and "customs" of the nations (Jeremiah 10:2–3). These ways and customs have replaced the worldview of the Bible with a new idolatrous hybrid worldview. This worldview has changed not just our thinking, but our behavior. And like Israel, we are largely unaware of our idolatry.

As Hitler's minister of munitions, Albert Speer was the chief designer of the Nazi war regime. After the war, he was questioned in his prison cell as to why he and other Germans had not recognized Hitler for who he was. Speer's answer is telling: "One seldom recognizes the devil when he is putting his hand on your shoulder."

Familiar evil is dangerous evil, all the more dangerous because we do not recognize it as such. The purpose of this chapter is to describe our own idolatrous familiar evil and expose how it has infiltrated the church.

Culture Has Introduced Idolatry to the Church

For both Israel and the church, culture is the medium that has introduced idolatry. *The Oxford English Dictionary* defines culture as: "A particular form or type of intellectual development. Also, the civilization, customs, artistic achievements, etc., of a people, especially at a certain stage of its development or history."

All cultures embody a system of values, truth, and morality, which produces a worldview that informs its people how to live. Following the Torah created a culture for Old Testament Israel; following Baal or other ancient deities created a different culture. Mixing the pagan culture/religion with the culture/religion of Old Testament Israel corrupted Israel without improving pagan culture and is one of the reasons for the commandment prohibiting idolatry. Ironically, God used the nations whose cultures Israel loved to judge her idolatry.

But despite this warning, over the centuries, the church has wedded herself to a pagan culture antithetical to Christ and Christianity. The result has been the same as it was for Israel: the church has been corrupted and the culture unchanged.

If you doubt the power and influence of our culture upon the church, consider the following thought experiment. Imagine a human being living alone on another planet. Jesus reveals Himself to him, and the man believes in Him. Jesus gives him a Bible, and the man reads, understands and assimilates it, becoming a fervent, if isolated, follower of our Lord. Jesus then asks the man if he would like to visit Earth, where biblical events took place and Christ is building His church. The man tingles in anticipation of witnessing firsthand the brethren's love for one another and the lost, their sacrificial lives of obedience to His commandments, and their hunger for the Word. He eagerly longs to talk with the young unmarried, who have kept themselves pure until their wedding day (1 Corinthians 6:18–20), and the married, whose marriages endure for life through good times and bad (Matthew 19:3–9). He expects to watch the church lovingly discipline the unrepentant sinner, seeking his restoration (Matthew 18:15–20; 1 Corinthians 5:5; 2 Corinthians 2:5–11). He anticipates that husbands will unswervingly be subject to Christ, heading their homes, loving their wives and washing them with the Word as Christ did the church (Ephesians

5:23–30). He supposes that wives will in turn submit to their husbands in the same way as the church submits to Christ (Ephesians 5:22), remaining silent in church with covered heads, asking their own husbands at home for instruction and clarification of the message taught by one of the church's prophets (1 Corinthians 14:34–35, 11:2–16).

This, of course, is not what he sees. Indeed you may take offense at some of the practices described above. But I assure you that all of them are commanded in the New Testament. Why is our alien brother chagrinned at what he sees, and why do we take offense at much of what the Bible so plainly teaches?

Of course, the simplest answer to this question is our sin. But I suggest that sin infects not only individuals but cultures as well. Further, sin's powerful effect on whole cultures causes it to become "familiar evil," magnifying the power of the discipline of delusion.

The Greek poet Pindar wrote, "Culture is lord of all." Most of us Christians would deny that culture is our lord. But in fact all of us are far more profoundly influenced by culture than we care to admit or may be aware of. We assimilate the ideas of our culture from infancy to death, beginning with our families, our schools, our friends, our churches, the arts, the media and a host of other influences, which combined we call culture. None of us reads the Bible without a cultural bias.

We Must Learn to Detect These Cultural Influences

If the Bible is the timeless wisdom of God and culture is the transient foolish wisdom of man, how can we remove those aspects of our cultural bias that threaten our faith? After all, aspects of all cultures exist that, if not affirmed by the Bible, at least do not conflict with it, including the many areas where Scripture is silent.

The solution begins by reminding ourselves of God's question to Adam immediately after the Fall: "*Who* told you that you were naked?" (Genesis 3:11). In evaluating our own convictions, particularly when we read something in the Bible with which we disagree, we should always ask ourselves, "*Who* told me so?" If certain passages in the New Testament appear outdated to us, the answer is likely our culture. Even church leaders are susceptible to reinterpreting passages of Scripture to accommodate the culture, and we must ask this question of everything we are taught, regardless of the source.

Paul tells us in 2 Corinthians 10:3–6 that the Christian's fight is both spiritual and ideological:

> For though we walk in the flesh, we do not war according to the flesh, for the weapons of our warfare are not of the flesh, but divinely powerful for the destruction of fortresses. We are destroying speculations and every lofty thing raised up against the knowledge of God, and we are taking every thought captive to the obedience of Christ.

The believer is called to engage in the spiritual battle of destroying any ideas contrary to God's truth.

When my kids were in high school, I asked them each night at the dinner table what they had learned in school. I then asked a follow up question: "Is that idea compatible with Scripture?" They may not have always enjoyed this little exercise, but the habit has served them well in filtering the ideas of both the world and the church. Because this is so essential to the preservation of our faith, my purpose is to dissect the ideas of Western culture and trace them back to their origins so we can understand who is telling us what we believe, and how these lies have led the church into idolatry.

Culture's Influence on the Church Is Ideological

The key difference between our idolatry and Israel's idolatry is that ours is populated by ideas rather than graven images. As we mentioned in the last chapter, this parallels the difference in emphasis of the two religions, with Judaism emphasizing the external sacrificial system, and Christianity emphasizing the internal transformation of the soul by the renewing of the mind (Romans 12:2).

But it also reflects the difference in the cultures of the two worlds into which each was born. In Old Testament times, pagan idolatry informed the cultures of the nations. But when Christianity emerged, it entered a culture that was growing tired of its gods. The ancient Greeks had already developed a system of philosophy that enabled man to determine how best to live grounded in human reason alone. Socrates, Plato, and Aristotle lived right after the completion of the Old Testament, and their goal was to do for themselves apart from the Law what God had done for Israel with the Law: to show people how to live. Paganism was already dying, and the church was born into a world increasingly ruled by human reason.

The church's philandering with the idolatry of human reason goes back to its very beginning. Early Christianity faced three primary obstacles: 1) Judaism, 2) paganism, and 3) philosophy. The Judaizers posed a strong threat to the early church, but the Jerusalem council (recounted in Acts 15), the writings of Paul, and the rapid influx of Gentiles into the church quickly neutralized them. The pagan idolatry of Greece and Rome was frequently cited as a danger in Paul's epistles, but by the end of the fourth century, as the Roman Empire crumbled, it was largely eliminated as well. In fact, it is remarkable that, unlike Israel, the church showed little interest in religious syncretism. If the early Christians were tempted to merge Christianity with pagan gods, we find little evidence of it in the historical record.

However, the church demonstrated a great deal of interest in fusing Christianity to Greek philosophy, especially Platonism. Indeed the first heresy was Gnosticism, a fusion of Plato and Christianity. But in its insistence that the way to God was through secret knowledge rather than faith in the death and resurrection of Jesus Christ, the church fathers easily identified Gnosticism as heresy and excised it. But the early church did not see other elements of Greek philosophy as a threat, instead considering them a friend. So philosophy became a handmaiden to theology. In this way, the church embraced and preserved the culture of the nations, in so doing producing what we now know as Western culture.

The Root of Western Culture Is Christian Syncretism

Western culture was born of two springs—what might be called Revelation, on the one hand, and Reason on the other. By Revelation, I mean the God-revealed religions of Judaism and Christianity. By Reason, I mean Greek philosophy, grounded in human reason and experience, which evolved from Socrates, Plato and Aristotle into the modern ideologies of scientific philosophy, secularism, and cultural Marxism, which we will discuss later. These two sources initially developed independently, then fused in the Middle Ages, and with the Enlightenment again resumed separate paths. The accompanying chart outlines this fusion and later separation.

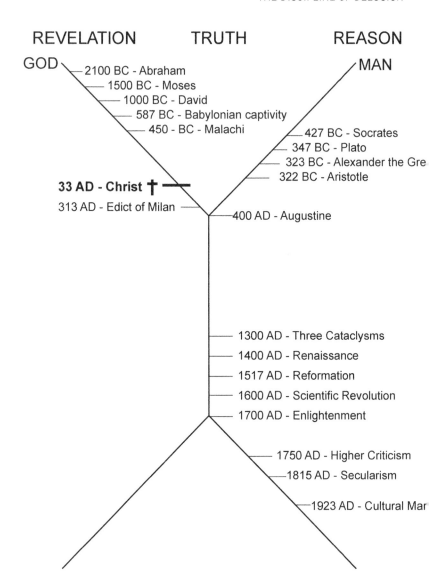

A History of Western Thought—The Synthesis of Revelation with Reason/Philosophy

Furthermore, Christian theologians deliberately synthesized Christianity first to Plato and later to Aristotle, a synthesis which lasted from roughly AD 400 to AD 1700. Reason and Revelation separated again during the eighteenth century Enlightenment, when intellectuals intentionally determined to free Reason from what they perceived to be the antiquated and restraining influence of religion, particularly Christianity.

The Reason side of the equation derived initially from Greek philosophy. As previously noted, the ancient Greeks did not associate knowledge and morality with their gods. Instead, they looked to themselves for these answers, creating philosophy, an endeavor to ground all knowledge and morality in human reason. This empowered man to become the final word on all matters of morality and knowledge. In this sense, man could return to the Tree of the Knowledge of Good and Evil, becoming god and claiming for himself the promise of the serpent, "For God knows that in the day you eat from it your eyes will be opened, and you will be like God, knowing good and evil" (Genesis 3:5). A worldview sprang from this philosophy, and the Reason side of Western culture was born.

Ancient Greek culture had many merits from which we still benefit—Aristotle's logic and the idea of democracy come quickly to mind—and the early church fathers recognized these merits and began using Greek philosophy as an aid to theology. This began early in church history and is most well-developed in the writings of Origen, Clement of Alexandria, and Augustine. The latter used the writings of Plato to explain many aspects of theology, including the Trinity. Plato's writings also provided inspiration for his idea of the City of God. Instead of a utopian society ruled by philosopher kings, the church would establish and rule a utopian society here on earth. The early church believed it could safely incorporate these seemingly innocuous ideas into Christian thinking by accepting the good in philosophy and rejecting anything unbiblical.

Syncretism is Folly

So what is wrong with this approach?

The theologians failed to heed Paul's admonition to the Corinthians in chapters 1–3 of his first letter:

> Indeed Jews ask for signs, and Greeks search for wisdom; but we preach Christ crucified, to Jews a stumbling block, and to Gentiles foolishness, but to those who are called, both Jews and Greeks, Christ the power of God and the wisdom of God. Because the foolishness of God is wiser than men, and the weakness of God is stronger than men ... God has chosen the foolish things of the world to shame the wise, and God has chosen the weak things of the world to shame the things which are strong, and the base things of the world and the despised, God has chosen, the things that are not, that He might nullify the things that are ...

that your faith should not rest on the wisdom of men, but on the power of God (1 Corinthians 1:22–25, 27–28; 2:5).

Paul explains that the wisdom of the world, the very best that human reason has to offer, is foolishness. It is incompatible with and has been nullified by the wisdom of God. Accordingly, he commands in 1 Corinthians 3:18, "Let no man deceive himself. If any man among you thinks that he is wise in this age, let him become foolish that he may become wise." In other words, we must unlearn the wisdom of the world if we wish to learn the wisdom of God.

He issues a similar warning in Colossians 2:8 and takes it a step further:

See to it that no one takes you captive through philosophy and empty deception, according to the tradition of men, according to the elementary principles of the world, rather than according to Christ.

Paul suggests here a similar concept to Jeremiah's discipline of delusion: learning the philosophical traditions of men leads to deception.

By ignoring Paul's admonitions, the early church did indeed become deceived, and this syncretism yielded unintended consequences. The problem with this fusion was less the content of Greek philosophy per se, which had relative merits. The problem was that the underlying premise of Greek philosophy (unaided human reason is a reliable guide to truth) was also incorporated. In doing so, the church unintentionally validated the primacy of human reason. Either reason is authoritative or revelation is authoritative. Over the centuries, the temptation to defer to unaided reason rather than the Bible proved too great for the church. Reason's first order is to understand revelation; but its second order is to subordinate itself to that revelation. But in today's church, revelation must subordinate itself to human reason. This is utterly incompatible with the Bible.

Like the builders of the Tower of Babel, Plato and the other Greek philosophers were driven by the idea of a man-made utopia, a dream that resides in every human heart. The quest for utopia is in fact a quest for autonomy, for a perfect world governed by man rather than God. By incorporating Greek philosophy, the church unwittingly validated this quest for autonomy, not realizing it was signing its own death warrant.

The unintended consequences of the church's embrace of Greek philosophy began to unfold with the Enlightenment. The medieval church was by no means above reproach, disobeying God as often as it obeyed Him. Nevertheless, during medieval times, Christianity served as a buttress against the extreme humanism that lay at the heart of Greek philosophy. Man as the master of his own destiny is an intoxicating poison, but this impulse was partially checked by the strong influence of the church. Thus for many centuries the church seemed to safely use philosophy as the handmaiden of theology; but she failed to anticipate that the handmaiden would slay her mistress.

Over the tumultuous fourteenth through seventeenth centuries, the church's authority was slowly fractured by numerous forces, including the Black Death, the Babylonian captivity of the church, the Hundred Years' War, the Renaissance, the Reformation, and the Scientific Revolution. These 400 years culminated in the Enlightenment, when intellectuals broke free from the restraints of Christianity, and human reason once again assumed the throne upon which Plato had placed her.

In this new world, no room remained for Christ. The collapse of the church's influence exposed man's naked longing to build a utopia based on human reason and experience alone. In violating Paul's admonitions, the church legitimized and sustained the seeds of its own destruction. Once the Enlightenment demolished the church's authority, it left philosophy as the only system of thought that anyone, including the church, would take seriously.

Reason, now unbridled by Christianity, was free to roam wherever she wished, and roam she did! The Enlightenment was a nuanced rather than a monolithic movement. Branches included the moderate Enlightenment of the Scientific Revolution, the Scottish

Enlightenment of Thomas Reid's Common Sense, the empirical British Enlightenment of Hume and Locke, and finally the radical French Enlightenment.

Over time, the radical movement grew stronger and exerted increasing influence. It aimed to establish and practice what Whittaker Chambers in *Witness* dubbed "the second oldest faith," the replacement of God by man as promised by the serpent in Genesis 3:5.[1] The second oldest religion, which had been suppressed since Babel by both true and false religions, was now finally able to establish man as the last false god.

As we noted before, coveting is a form of idolatry (Ephesians 5:5; Colossians 3:5). The second oldest religion is idolatrous in that man covets what belongs to God alone—the headship of the human race. The question is, who defines for humanity what is best for us? In the aftermath of the Enlightenment, the answer is man himself.

Syncretism Has Deluded the Church

The church has drunk deeply from the well of the Enlightenment despite the movement's hostility toward it. One of the Enlightenment's most pernicious influences on the church has been its philosophy of doubt. While the foundation of Christianity is faith, the foundation of the Enlightenment is doubt. Cartesian doubt, popularized by René Descartes, is a systematic process of being skeptical about (or doubting) the truth of one's beliefs in order to test their validity. This idea was imported into Christian theology and dubbed "higher criticism." Initially authored by the German biblical scholar Friedrich Schleiermacher (although many other theologians were involved), their intent was to take the methods of science and rationalism and apply them to the scriptures.

One of the results of this criticism has been a redefinition of what the modern church considers to be true and moral, thereby invalidating many biblical teachings. Prior to the influence of higher criticism, the scriptures stood in authority over man and his reason. Reason's duty was to subordinate itself to revelation. The higher critics, in contrast, stood in judgment over the scriptures, doubting their veracity unless they could "prove" it to the satisfaction of reason. Prior to higher criticism, reason bowed the knee to revelation; afterwards, revelation bowed the knee to reason.

On higher criticism's chopping block have been scriptural teachings on the role of the sexes, proscriptions on sexuality, and church discipline. The hypothetical alien's surprise at the state of the modern church owes much to the revisionist activities of higher criticism. We will explore more fully in later chapters how the culture has influenced our beliefs on these subjects.

My point is not that that we have broken these commandments and our ancestors did not, for they surely did, but rather that we no longer consider such teachings to be valid. We cannot be called to repentance because, in our own eyes, we have done nothing wrong—there is nothing from which to repent! Disobedience and rebellion are not equivalent. Disobedience involves breaking a commandment; rebellion entails questioning its validity.

The lie that there is nothing from which to repent is the essence of the discipline of delusion! I remind you of Israel and the golden calf. They committed what seems to be obvious idolatry, but in their eyes they were worshipping the LORD!

The book of Jeremiah describes this delusion's power and destruction before the Babylonian captivity. The people were incredulous that God was accusing them of idolatry:

> "When you tell this people all these words … they will say to you, 'For what reason has the LORD declared all this great calamity against us? And what is our iniquity, or what is our sin which we have committed against the LORD our God?' Then you are to say to them, 'It is because your forefathers have forsaken Me,' declares the LORD, 'and have followed other gods and served them and bowed down to them; but Me they have forsaken and have not kept My law" (Jeremiah 16:10–11).

Instead of wedding the LORD to Baal, Christianity has wedded Christ with the religion of man, currently in the form of scientific philosophy, secularism, and cultural Marxism. Biblically speaking, the church has been taken "captive through philosophy" despite Paul's warning (Colossians 2:8).

Although Paul does not address philosophy extensively in the New Testament, this does not negate its importance to the church. I remind you of the Old Testament teaching on faith. Paul, James and the author of Hebrews quote one or both of only two Old Testament passages on faith, Genesis 15:6, "Then [Abraham] believed in the LORD; and He reckoned it to him as righteousness," and Habakkuk 2:4, "But the righteous will live by his faith." These New Testament writers insist that based on these two verses, righteousness was always by faith and not the works of the Law.

Were I an Old Testament Jew, I doubt very much that I would have picked these two verses and given them the importance and centrality the New Testament writers ascribed to them, particularly in light of the volume of words written about the Law and obedience. I do not cite this to prove that Colossians 2:8 is as important as I believe it to be but rather to demonstrate that no necessary connection exists between the importance of a verse and the number of times the Scripture repeats it. Remember Moses' admonition not to add to the commandments of God nor take away from them; the warning was made once, and yet Jesus excoriates the Pharisees for violating this command. God calls us to heed all of

His warnings regardless of how many times He gives
them.

Syncretism Denies the Authority of Christ

Like the Pharisees, however, the discipline of
delusion has led the church to add to and subtract
from the commandments of God, leading to a deadly
state of disobedience. Jesus warns His followers in
Matthew 7:21–23:

> "Not everyone who says to Me, 'Lord, Lord,' will
> enter the kingdom of heaven; but he who does
> the will of My Father who is in heaven. Many will
> say to Me on that day, 'Lord, Lord, did we not
> prophesy in Your name, and in Your name cast
> out demons, and in Your name perform many
> miracles?' And I will declare to them, 'I never
> knew you; depart from Me, you who practice
> lawlessness.'"

Jesus here tells us we cannot be assured of entrance
into heaven unless we do the will of His Father. Note with
me that, like the children of Israel, the people to whom
He refers in this passage are deluded. They think they are
obedient followers of the Lord; Christ does not. From
Paul's writings we know that the ground, or basis, for
our salvation is the blood of Christ alone, and faith is the
condition for receiving that salvation. But the evidence

for that faith is obedience. Biblical faith does not exist unless we have broken our wills and submitted to the Father. No man this side of eternity other than Christ has exhibited perfect obedience. But His expectation is that we believe everything that He tells us, acknowledging all of His commands as true and endeavoring with all of our beings to obey them. He is telling us that He is not our Lord because we call Him so, but when we submit to His authority to define truth and goodness for us.

James supports the essential role of obedience by saying that "faith without works is dead" (James 2:26). John reiterates, "By this we know that we have come to know Him, if we keep His commandments. The one who says, 'I have come to know Him' and does not keep His commandments, is a liar, and the truth is not in him" (1 John 2:3–4). *Liar* is not a word we use in polite company, but John uses it to emphasize the importance of keeping His commandments.

But the modern church has ignored all these warnings and instead practices an obedience-optional Christianity. This conduct is a direct result of uncritically embracing the religion of man that reemerged with the Enlightenment. We are children of the Enlightenment and its aftermath, and we read the Bible from that perspective. We have fashioned God in our own image, and He now serves us on our terms rather than the other way around.

Pastor and author A. W. Tozer, in his final essay before his death in 1963 entitled "The Waning Authority of Christ in the churches," summarizes the state of the post-Enlightenment church:

> Jesus Christ has today almost no authority at all among the groups that call themselves by His name . . . . The present position of Christ in the gospel churches may be likened to that of a king in a limited, constitutional monarchy. The king (sometimes depersonalized by the term "the Crown") is in such a country no more than a traditional rallying point, a pleasant symbol of unity and loyalty much like a flag or a national anthem. He is lauded, feted and supported, but his real authority is small. Nominally he is head over all, but in every crisis someone else makes the decisions.

He describes the means of our enemy's successful assault on the modern church:

> In the Western world the enemy has forsworn violence. He comes against us no more with sword and fagot; he now comes smiling, bearing gifts. He raises his eyes to heaven and swears that he too believes in the faith of our fathers, but his real purpose is to destroy that faith, or at least to modify it to such an extent that it is no longer the supernatural thing it once was. He

comes in the name of philosophy or psychology or anthropology, and with sweet reasonableness urges us to rethink our historic position, to be less rigid, more tolerant, more broadly understanding.

He concludes with the following charge:

What, then, are we to do? Each one of us must decide, and there are at least three possible choices. One is to rise up in shocked indignation and accuse me of irresponsible reporting. Another is to nod general agreement with what is written here but take comfort in the fact that there are exceptions and we are among the exceptions. The other is to go down in meek humility and confess that we have grieved the Spirit and dishonored our Lord in failing to give Him the place His Father has given Him as Head and Lord of the Church. Either the first or the second will but confirm the wrong. The third if carried out to its conclusion can remove the curse. The decision lies with us.

Syncretism Leads to Apostasy
The natural fulfillment of the discipline of delusion in the church is apostasy. Christianity began when Israel rejected Christ, and it will end when the church rejects

Him. Alluding to the return of the Lord in 2 Thessalonians 2:3, 8–12, Paul writes,

> Let no one in any way deceive you, for it will not come unless the apostasy comes first, and the man of lawlessness is revealed, the son of destruction . . . . Then that lawless one will be revealed whom the Lord will slay with the breath of His mouth and bring to an end by the appearance of His coming; that is, the one whose coming is in accord with the activity of Satan, with all power and signs and false wonders, and with all the deception of wickedness for those who perish, because they did not receive the love of the truth so as to be saved. And for this reason God will send upon them a deluding influence so that they will believe what is false, in order that they all may be judged who did not believe the truth, but took pleasure in wickedness.

The deluding influence referred to in these verses is the same as that which led Old Testament Israel from the LORD to the idols and finally to judgment. "However, when the Son of Man comes, will He find faith on earth?" (Luke 18:8) is not a picture of the Church Triumphant! We have been warned—I plead with us not to ignore these warnings! He is gracious to forgive, but we cannot repent of what we do not call sin!

In the next chapters, we will look in more detail at some of the humanistic ideologies embraced by the church in the aftermath of the Enlightenment: the philosophy underlying modern science, which provides a rival truth system to the Bible; secular humanism, which provides a man-centered morality to replace Christianity; and cultural Marxism, which has set out to destroy the church and all other traditional authority.

CHAPTER 5

The Church and Science

IF GOD SUPPLIES His people with both knowledge and morality, modern science challenges His divine right to define knowledge—that is, what is real and what is true.

Science is not good or bad in and of itself. It is a highly productive discipline for discovering the laws of nature and then using those laws to our advantage. But for the Christian, it is illegitimate as a system for determining ultimate truth because ultimate truth is spiritual, not natural. Scientism, not science per se, is my concern. By scientism I mean the omnipotent and exclusive knowledge claims that some make for science, whereby knowledge claims from other sources, such as the Bible, are marginalized and ridiculed. I reject this view completely. For the purposes of simplicity, I will refer to scientism as science in this chapter, but it is this movement specifically and not science in general that is the subject of discussion.

John William Draper voices the disdain proponents of scientism hold for religion in *History of the Conflict Between Religion and Science*:

> The history of Science is not a mere record of isolated discoveries; it is a narrative of the conflict of two contending powers, the expansive force of the human intellect on the one side, and the compression arising from traditionary faith and human interests on the other.

Science as a truth system is growing increasingly militant and is contributing to the destruction of the church. Many of the accounts and stories of the Bible have been called into question by science, and the conflict between science and the Bible is frequently cited by atheists as a reason they do not believe. Furthermore, scientific theories such as evolution and the Big Bang have marginalized religion by claiming no need for a Creator and depicting man as a solely physical being without a soul, similar to other animals.

As important as these specific disputes are, I do not intend to address them individually, but rather to more broadly question the legitimacy of the knowledge claims made by science. To do so, we must explore the philosophical basis of its knowledge claims, and how, along with secular humanism and cultural Marxism, it has created a culture with a worldview contrary to the Bible.

Science offers a tempting alternative to the biblical worldview because of its tremendous success. The technological and intellectual achievements of modern science are unsurpassed by any other field of human inquiry, which often causes us to forget or neglect the spiritual. The body of knowledge produced by science is breathtaking and surely the crown jewel of human intellectual pursuits. I greatly respect and admire science and the men and women who have contributed so prodigiously to it. But tragically, we have learned this treasure trove of natural knowledge at the expense of our souls.

Science is rooted in philosophy, and as with all truth systems, is founded on a basic set of presuppositions. For the rest of this chapter I will examine seven broad points about scientific assumptions and their effect on the church. These scientific claims oppose the bible, and their effects on the culture have led the church to lose its soul by trading the eternal for the temporal. In this, the church rather than science bears the most blame.

Science and the Bible Disagree on the Nature of Reality

Science's claims about the basic nature of reality differ from the biblical understanding. Both science and the Bible seek to answer the question, how exactly do things work in the universe and what is the basic nature of reality?

Science and the Bible agree on two important points: 1) A reality exists which underlies experience; and 2) Nobody experiences that reality. But the Bible and science disagree violently on the nature of that reality.

For example, science reveals that the earth rotates on its axis at approximately 1,000 miles per hour at the equator while it revolves around the sun at approximately 66,000 miles per hour. This is reality, but we do not experience the reality of this motion. I am writing this on a desk, which I experience as solid. It holds up my computer and supports my arms that rest on it. Nonetheless, science tells us that the desk is mostly empty space, with the atoms of the desk having central nuclei and peripheral electrons held together by electromagnetic attraction, with mostly empty space between them. But I don't experience this empty space; instead I experience a solid table.

These and many other examples all point to the same conclusion that a reality underlies ordinary experience which we do not directly experience. The crucial question and point of divergence between science and the Bible is, what is the nature of that reality?

The scientific account claims that the reality we do not experience is naturalistic and materialistic only. This view is termed "scientific materialism," which according to *The American Heritage Dictionary of the English Language*, is "the philosophical opinion that physical matter in its movements and modifications is the only reality and that everything in the universe, including thought, feeling,

mind, and will, can be explained in terms of physical laws"
(Ed. William Morris, 1973).

To my understanding, the Bible does not dispute
much of the scientific account with one major
exception—it insists that a transcendent spiritual reality,
which we do not ordinarily perceive, underlies all experience
and superintends the natural realm. Furthermore, that
underlying spiritual reality is both moral and our home!
Life must therefore be understood in primarily spiritual
and moral rather than natural terms.

We have discussed this concept previously, but
because it is critically important to understanding the
conflict between science and the Bible, I want to offer two
more examples of the biblical teaching that the spiritual
superintends the natural.

The first is stated in Jeremiah 14:22, "Are there any
among the idols of the nations who give rain? Or can the
heavens grant showers? Is it not Thou, O LORD our God?
Therefore we hope in Thee, for Thou art the one who hast
done all these things." Three options for the cause of rain
are offered: 1) the pagan idols; 2) the heavens; and 3) God.
The first option is the pagan position. The second option
is the scientific position, namely that nature is a closed,
self-sustaining system impervious to outside influences.
Jeremiah says that the first two options are simply wrong.

So who is right, the Scripture or science? As we
established earlier, however we answer this question for
ourselves, we answer by faith—we cannot prove our

answer. I only point out that science and the Scripture cannot both be true on this foundational point. I am not suggesting that no naturalistic mechanisms exist, but only that whatever those naturalistic mechanisms may be, they are superintended and even sometimes circumvented by God.

The Bible is clear that God not only set those mechanisms in motion in the first place—and can interrupt them any time He pleases—but that through Christ, He continues to command that they operate. Hebrews 1:3 tells us that Jesus Christ "upholds all things by the word of His power." Colossians 1:17 similarly teaches us that "in Him, all things hold together." In other words, the movements of the weather and the oceans, the spinning of the earth, the forces of gravity and electromagnetism and everything else only continue because Christ commands them to do so.

A second illustration of this is seen in the book of Revelation, which we have already cited. In chapter five God the Father holds a scroll with seven seals which can be opened only by Christ. Whenever a seal is opened it is followed by a calamity on earth, and that calamity is mediated by an angel. The question we must answer: is this only true for the end times or is this a statement about the nature of all of history? Based on the verses cited above and previously, I suggest that this portrait of spiritual causality is not unique to Revelation but rather the blueprint for all that happens on earth.

Therefore, my quarrel is not with the scientific method, which is a valid means of studying God's universe, but with science as a philosophical system or worldview. As a philosophical system, it assumes that natural phenomena have only natural causes, which conflicts sharply with the presupposition of the Bible that the spiritual superintends the natural.

Science Studies Creation Rather Than the Creator

Science as a philosophical system is further objectionable because it relies on creation rather than the Creator as its source of truth. Science began as a branch of philosophy just as did ethics and metaphysics. In fact, the term "metaphysics" refers to Aristotle's "Physics," the study of the physical or natural world, and means "after physics." Early scientists were first called "natural philosophers," i.e. philosophers who studied nature.

Because the scientific enterprise sprang from a Christian culture, many early scientists were Christians. It has been observed that science would not have been possible without belief in a lawful, immutable God who governs the universe through rationally comprehensible, unchanging, and therefore predictable, laws.

Science, then, is the systematic and often mathematical study of the material universe and its laws. Richard M. Weaver notes in his book, *Ideas Have Consequences,* that science "encouraged a careful study of nature . . . on the supposition that by her acts she revealed her essence."[1]

In this, science grounds knowledge in creation, while Christianity grounds it in the Creator and His revelation of Himself through the Bible.

Creation teaches much about God and man (Romans 1:20); the Bible teaches more. Further, science studies not just creation, but *fallen* creation. Therefore whatever we can conclude from creation is less reliable than what we can learn from the Creator.

To put science in biblical context, remember Colossians 2:8: "See to it no one take you captive through philosophy and empty deception, according to the tradition of men, according to the elementary principles of the world, rather than according to Christ." The "elementary principles of the world" refers to the natural world, which to reiterate, is the object of scientific inquiry.

Knowledge of the natural or temporal world is entirely different from knowledge of the eternal or spiritual world. Hebrews 12:26–28 prophesies:

And His voice shook the earth [at Sinai], but now He has promised, saying, "Yet once more I will shake not only the earth, but also the heaven." And this expression, "Yet once more," denotes the removing of those things which can be shaken, as of created things, in order that those things which cannot be shaken may remain. Therefore, since we receive a kingdom which cannot be shaken, let us show gratitude.

The present natural world will be shaken and removed. Therefore, knowledge of it is of less value than knowledge of the spiritual world.

Science Claims That Nature Is a Closed System

But scientific philosophy denies the existence of the spiritual realm, and therefore must derive all its explanations of causality from nature alone. Nature in this context refers to that which can be detected by our ordinary human senses and/or scientific instruments, which are extensions of those senses. Science presupposes that nature is a closed system, and all natural phenomena must be explained only by other natural phenomena. So where did this assumption that nature is a closed system originate?

Men like Bacon, Descartes, Galileo, and Newton were well-known central figures of the seventeenth century Scientific Revolution. However, the most foundational philosophical presuppositions necessary for their work and for the modern scientific enterprise go back further still to Adelard of Bath in the twelfth century.

Adelard suggested that the job of science is to describe natural phenomena in terms of their causes, of which two principles must be assumed to be true: 1) All natural phenomena must be explained only by natural causes; and 2) Nature is a closed system, that is, no forces outside of nature may be invoked to explain a natural phenomenon.

For example, a rainbow appears after rain. What causes it? Adelard's two principles disallow an explanation that God placed it there as a promise to never again flood the earth (Genesis 9:12–16).

This draws into focus an important point. If we use Adelard's two presuppositions to "do science" and agree that we are using them for that purpose only, then no conflict with Scripture exists. The problem arises when we use these presuppositions and add the separate judgment, "they are true." This, then, becomes a significant departure from Scripture.

I remind you again that presuppositions by their very definition cannot be proven. What proof can one offer that nature is a closed system and no forces outside it exist or operate? How could Adelard or a modern scientist know this is true? What experiment can verify it? These questions can only be answered by faith. And that is true for the scientist and the Christian alike! The thesis of Scripture is that God rules His creation, from big events (Deuteronomy 32:39; Isaiah 45:5–7; Lamentations 3:37–38) to small events (Proverbs 16:33; Matthew 10:29–30).

But by denying the involvement of spiritual causes, the scientific explanation of causality is woefully inadequate. It is instructive to look at scientific causality through the grid of Aristotle's well-developed thinking on causes. He proposed that there are four aspects of causation: 1) material, 2) formal, 3) efficient, and most importantly, 4) final causes.

Consider again the cause of a rainbow. The material causes are water and light; the formal causes are the laws of physics, which govern the interaction of light with water; while the efficient cause is the light of the sun after the rain of a thunderstorm. What is the final cause? For Aristotle, this was the most important aspect because the final cause answers the question, "why?"

Employing Aristotle's logic, science explains the first three but not the final and most important. The Bible does explain the final cause of rainbows, although it chooses not to decode many other natural phenomena. But God does tell us the ultimate "why," that all things are created for Christ and will be summed up in Him (Colossians 1:16; Ephesians 1:10).

The point, then, is not to validate Aristotle's thinking on causality, which as human wisdom is flawed since it fails to understand that even material, formal and efficient causes are under God's direct supervision. Rather the point is that, biblically speaking, God is the final cause of all things, and that whether or not He tells us every why, His purposes are served. Therefore, we can never understand the true cause of the universe or any event in history if we merely study creation.

Scientific Authority: Human Reason

Scientific philosophy believes that it can arrive at truth without invoking God or any other final cause. Human reason is the only authority it claims to require.

This brings us to a broader philosophical question in man's quest for knowledge: what is really meant when a discipline (such as science, philosophy or religion) claims to know that something is true? Are our claims to knowledge (in this case scientific knowledge, though the question applies to all knowledge claims) transcendent, i.e. are they universal, necessary and certain, and True with a capital *T*? Or is our knowledge particular, and therefore contingent, open to doubt, and subject to revision upon new discoveries?

Why does this matter? It matters because if scientific claims are merely interpretations of experience rather than claims to universal, necessary and certain knowledge, then science does not offer a rival truth system to the Bible. Science can acceptably offer a materialistic explanation of particular experiences that might change as new experiences are examined; but it cannot acceptably offer a worldview or explanation of things as they really are. In other words, it may offer a pattern of observations so long as it makes no claims to universal truth.

But this is not what science wishes for itself. It insists on being taken more seriously. It ambitiously asserts that it offers the *only* rational worldview for thinking men to believe—a worldview devoid of God. In doing so, it has brought humanity right back to the Tree of the Knowledge of Good and Evil.

From the very beginning, God used the Tree to place the knowledge problem front and center for humanity.

How can a man know anything is true? God tells us that we have three potential sources of knowledge: Himself, the serpent, and human reason. God has ordained that as finite beings, we are necessarily dependent on a source outside ourselves to understand truth.

Science not only refutes this claim, it denies the very existence of God and the serpent. Instead, it views the Tree, not from the spiritual and moral perspective of God's commandments, but from the perspective of human reason and materialism. It studies the Tree and says, "This looks good for food, and is a delight to the eyes, and is useful to make one wise. Let's test it and see what we can learn from it."

Science falsely claims that determining truth for ourselves is more reliable than trusting God because science can prove its answers. In my career as a dermatologist, we physicians were obsessed with scientific evidence. We looked to scientific literature to "prove" that a particular medication worked or that a certain immune imbalance or infection was the cause of a particular disease. Of course, in many cases, the literature was wrong. But despite its failures, the scientific community continues to operate on the assumption that the scientific method reliably ascertains truth because it claims we will continue to learn from and correct our errors. Science ignores the fact that, if that "truth" must be continuously revised with new information, it cannot be universal and transcendent—it is a theory and not a truth.

Scientists cannot prove their claims are universal and transcendent any more than can the believer of the Bible. In fact, the scientific method demonstrates the reverse, that science's claims are incomplete and constantly subject to revision. The result is what the Bible has long taught—men must walk by faith and not sight/knowledge—whether we acknowledge it or not. God has drawn a veil over our eyes. All of us are forced to base our lives on presuppositions that we cannot prove, and this knowledge problem, which God built into the fabric of our existence, is illustrative of that fact.

Science Mistakes "What Works" For "What Is True"

Scientific philosophy thinks so highly of its ability to discern truth because it has mistaken "what works" for "what is true." As Richard Weaver observes, in scientific theory, "we see 'fact' substituted for 'truth.'"[2] So we must ask ourselves, if science is not true (with a capital *T*), then how has it been so astonishingly successful?

Let's examine this question through the grid of a statement made by Stephen Hawking, the great cosmologist, in an interview with Diane Sawyer. "There is a fundamental difference between religion, which is based on authority, and science, which is based on reason and experience. Science will win because it works."

Hawking is a brilliant physicist but a pedestrian philosopher. Though a number of objections could be made to his statement, I only want to examine the "it works" portion of Hawking's remark. "It works" and "it is true" are not synonyms.

For example, if I drive to your house in my car and you question me about how my car functions, I am apt to reply that "it works," meaning it performs satisfactorily the function of delivering me safely to your house. But no matter how hard you press me, I will not say my car is "true" with a capital T. I won't, and neither will you, because we all understand that Truth is imbued with an eternal and transcendent character. In the parlance of the philosopher, Truth is universal, necessary and certain, and my car is none of these. In this we see that a thing can "work" while not necessarily being True.

This characteristic of working but not being true is found in many scientific theories as they have evolved over time. Isaac Newton's theory of gravity and motion is illustrative but by no means unique. The equations Newton's theory put forth were so successful and "true" for so long that though they were developed in the end of the seventeenth century, they were successfully used to send men to the moon and return them safely to Earth.

But is his theory really true? What were the presuppositions upon which he based it? Two presuppositions undergird Newton's theory: 1) Space is uniform in all directions; and 2) Time moves uniformly for all observers.

These seem to be very commonsense premises on which to build a theory—but how did Newton know they were true? Did he perform experiments in different parts of the universe to reach these conclusions? No, he assumed them to be true, and they were held to be so until Albert Einstein proffered his theory of relativity in 1915. According to Einstein, space is not uniform in all directions but is instead deformed by massive objects, and time does not run at the same pace in all circumstances but slows down as an object approaches the speed of light.

The fundamental assumptions (or presuppositions) of Newton's theory were proven false, but despite this, his equations continued to work under all but the most extreme conditions.[3] "What works" and "what is true" are not the same.

But I wish to make a second point about what works: just because it works does not mean it is the best solution. If you contract leprosy and see a qualified physician, he will give you a prescription for antibiotics (discovered through the use of science), and it will likely improve or cure your leprosy—it works! But it works better for Jesus to say, "Leper be cleansed," and be immediately healed! Similarly, if you lose your sight, medical science may be able to restore it, at least partially—it works. But it works better for Jesus to say, "Receive your sight"! The miracles of the Bible stand outside anything that science can explain because they are the evidence that the spiritual superintends the natural and that nature is not a closed system!

But more important still is the question of "what works" after death. Of necessity, science is mute on this point, whereas the Bible teaches that faith in Jesus Christ is the only thing that "works" after death. If we believe that to be true, then we must of necessity believe that He is the only One who truly "works" in this life as well!

A Flood of Information Drowns Knowledge of the Spiritual

If knowledge of what works cannot produce ultimate truth, then the vast flood of knowledge produced by science is, at best, a distraction in our quest for true knowledge.

As I briefly touched on earlier, knowledge of nature (scientific knowledge) and knowledge of spiritual things are two very different kinds of knowledge. The former is based on presuppositions which disallow references to anything spiritual and confine it to the observation of creation through reason and experience. The latter is based on the revelation of the Bible. Both are based on conflicting but unproved presuppositions. If Science with a capital *S* is true, then the Bible is false.

But if the Bible is true, then knowledge of the spiritual is infinitely more important than knowledge of nature, and understanding the soul more important than understanding the body. It is true that Scripture teaches that we can learn much about God through nature, but direct revelation from God through the medium of Scripture is vastly superior.

We live in a time when knowledge about the unimportant (nature) is exploding, while knowledge of the important (the spiritual) is in rapid decline. The Bible anticipated this. In Daniel 12:4, God foretells that in the end times, "knowledge will increase." How can knowledge increase?

Prior to the advent of science there was no answer to this question, but science has now become a key philosophical tool for the generation of knowledge, and this knowledge is choking us to death. T. S. Eliot, writing a century ago in "Choruses from the Rock," bemoaned this: "Where is the wisdom we have lost in knowledge? Where is the knowledge we have lost in information?" Computers and the Internet, two bequeathals of science, are both two-edged swords. They have made the acquisition of information very cheap but, as Eliot observes, information is not knowledge, and knowledge is not wisdom. When information is cheap, focus on what truly matters becomes very expensive.

Information is like water—we need it to live. But when it comes in the form of a flood or a tsunami it destroys. And information is indeed coming in the form of a flood or tsunami, and it is destroying our ability to think about anything important. As T. S. Eliot observed, we have "knowledge of words, and ignorance of the Word. All our knowledge brings us nearer to our ignorance, all our ignorance brings us nearer to death, but nearness to death no nearer to GOD." We must understand and escape this before it destroys our souls. Information becomes knowledge when we apply it, and knowledge becomes wisdom when it becomes a part of the fabric of our souls. But this process takes time and focus.

The Bible is clear—God placed us here on earth to develop our souls in preparation for eternity. Excess information causes us to think about details other than our souls. To the degree you can get a man to think about something other than his soul is the degree to which you can nudge a man away from Christ. We have nudged thinking about our souls, thinking about death, thinking about Christ, off the screen. If a man will talk about his soul or death, then you have the chance to talk to him about something important.

The Myth of Progress Causes Us to Neglect God's Commands

This explosion of knowledge has resulted in even more ominous change today, which the scriptures also anticipated. In 2 Thessalonians 2:3, Paul speaks about the return of Christ and the "man of lawlessness." "Let no one in any way deceive you, for it will not come unless the apostasy comes first, and the man of lawlessness is revealed, the son of destruction."

The apostasy occurs when the church no longer believes in Christ, and instead embraces "lawlessness." Lawlessness is the denial of God's law, and God's law is expressed in His Word through His commandments.

Although we may not be aware of it, Paul tells us that even though the "man of lawlessness" has not yet appeared, "the mystery of lawlessness is already at work" amongst us (verse 7). The biblical definition of a mystery is a spiritual truth that we are unaware of until God uncovers it. The gospel was a mystery until it was revealed in Christ (1 Corinthians 2:7); similarly, the future union of the Jews and Gentiles in one body was not disclosed until the debut of the church (Ephesians 3:4). It is no mystery that lawlessness exists in the world. The mystery is that lawlessness exists in the church.

The lawlessness in the church has unfolded in just the same manner as it did for the Pharisees: adding to and subtracting from the commandments of God. We in the modern church find a scripture that we like and then use it to disprove a portion of Scripture that we don't like! We look at commandments that counter our current culture, like women not leading men, and we say, "The people of the past were primitive and sexist. Now we know better." Like the serpent in the Garden, we are in essence saying, "Did God really say that?" Our problem is not disbelieving the scriptures in a wholesale fashion but rather believing what we find agreeable and discounting the rest.

How is this tendency related to the explosion of scientific knowledge? Scientific achievement and the theory of evolution combined with Marxist philosophy to create a myth of progress, causing us to believe that we know more than we actually do. We believe because our technology is better than our predecessors, we can also interpret the Scripture more accurately. In other words, we believe that our superior knowledge of nature translates into moral and spiritual superiority.

The myth of progress has come at the expense of developing the soul, leading instead to moral and spiritual degeneration. Distracted by a deluge of unimportant information, we neither know how to think nor what is worth thinking about, which is all the more dangerous because we live in a time when ideology is the new idolatry. Instead of being "transformed by the renewing of [our] mind[s]" (Romans 12:2), we conform to the world. Biblically illiterate and incapable of reasoning about the ideologies we embrace, we are driven instead by desire and passion. Professing to be wise, we have become fools, and God has given us over to the lusts of our hearts (Romans 1:22, 24). Yet mimicking the children of Israel, we refuse to repent. Like the adulterous woman of Proverbs 30:20, we "eat and wipe [our] mouth[s], and say, 'I have done no wrong.'" We cannot believe we could be wrong because of our arrogant conviction that we are smarter than our predecessors.

In summary, science is a system of thought based on unproven presuppositions; so is the Bible. The presuppositions of the two are mutually exclusive—they cannot both be true. Science has produced many discoveries that work spectacularly, and this success enamors us. But what works for the problem of sin, or what works after death? Only Scripture offers answers to these questions.

As a truth system, science tells me all I want to know except what matters most to me. How should I live my life? Why is it so difficult for me to live as I know I ought? Why am I here? What happens to me after I die? A truth system that offers no answers to these and similar questions is unworthy of a serious person. But despite its inadequacy, science has been widely accepted as an alternative source of truth to the Bible and has lent credence to the efforts of secularism to divorce morality from the Bible as well. In the next chapter, we will explore the tenets of secularism and how they have infiltrated the church.

CHAPTER 6

The Church and Secularism

SECULARISM IS THE coalescence and crystallization of mankind's endeavor to govern its own affairs without divine interference. It is not so much a well-defined philosophical system as a declaration of independence. Just as science provides the knowledge component necessary for man's autonomy, secularism supplies the moral dimension.

The Oxford English Dictionary defines *secularism* as: "The doctrine that morality should be based solely on regard to the well-being of mankind in the present life, to the exclusion of all considerations drawn from belief in God or in a future state."

This central aim of secularism is antithetical to the Bible in two critical ways: 1) It creates a new morality, defining good based on what mankind determines to be in his best interest, rather than the moral imperatives of God; and 2) It espouses an alternative worldview which only considers this present life in its determination of what that good looks like.

Despite this mutual incompatibility, in this chapter we will discuss how the church has, for all intents and purposes, become secular in its morality and worldview. We have done so by becoming temporally focused, no longer believing in eternal consequences for our actions here on earth. The unfortunate consequence of this secular view has been an increasing tendency in the church to break the commandments of God to secure temporal happiness, however transitory it might be.

The Philosophical Backbone of Secularism Concerns This Present Life

To identify how it has infiltrated the church, we must first understand secularism as a belief system. Secularism, like science and cultural Marxism, is a product of Enlightenment principles and cooperates with those philosophies quite closely.

The term *secularism* was coined by George Holyoake in the mid-nineteenth century, but a number of other thinkers were involved in developing its ideas during that period. For the purposes of simplicity, I will use the term secularism interchangeably with secular humanism.

It began as a movement to provide a new man-centered morality without reference to God or religious authority. Most of its early proponents didn't deny the validity of religion, but merely claimed that morality should be defined independently from it. In this sense, it is less a well-defined system than a bald assertion of man's autonomy on issues of morality.

Just as science denies a reality beyond nature, secularism's only concern is this present life rather than the afterlife. Without the anchor of eternal accountability to an absolute divine morality, it believes that the search for moral truth is adaptive (evolving based on circumstances rather than absolute) and is guided by reason, science, and experience. It defines ethics (doing good) as what enhances human well-being according to man's reason, and its chief virtue is tolerance.

Its goal is to promote human flourishing here on earth. It does so by establishing a purely humanistic morality governed only by earthly and temporal considerations. In this sense, it is a return to the Tree of the Knowledge of Good and Evil, enabling man to define morality for himself without reference to God's authority or our accountability to Him in the afterlife.

Secularism, like science, is believed by its adherents to be superior to religion because they believe faith is not required to accept it. But secularism is an ideology, and as such, it exhibits the limitations of all ideologies. According to *The Oxford English Dictionary*, an ideology is defined as "a systematic scheme of ideas, usually relating to politics or society, or the conduct of a class or group, and regarded as justifying actions, especially one that is held implicitly or adopted as a whole and maintained regardless of the course of events."

The last clause, "maintained regardless of the course of events," is revealing. Secularism is an ideology in that it is held uncritically and is irrefutable by any event, even if clinging to it leads to calamitous results! It is therefore an article of faith in a system that claims by its very definition to be true. Like science and cultural Marxism, secularism is no more objective than and requires as much faith as the religious systems it so disdains.

In this way, secularism is a religion—the most recent manifestation of the second oldest religion, whose god is man—an idolatrous religion at war with Christianity. Though many secularists would deny this charge, Justice Hugo Black referred to secular humanism as a religion in a Supreme Court ruling of 1961 in the case of *Torcaso v. Watkins*.

As we discussed in Chapter 3, "The Discipline of Delusion," idolatry includes both a worldview and a moral code, and secularism is no exception. Both its idolatrous worldview and attendant morality are central to understanding how it has infiltrated Christianity. Its worldview is confined to "the well-being of mankind in the present life," and its morality seeks to define good for mankind within this limited framework. Though it does not deny God's existence, it excludes Him from all moral considerations.

This omission of considerations regarding God and the afterlife renders its worldview incompatible with Christianity. The God of the Bible is moral, and He expects His people to conform to that morality! He further insists that failure to do so carries eternal consequences. Unfortunately, as secularism has grown in influence over our culture, it has replaced God's morality with the whims of men and removed Christianity from the public square with respect to moral conduct. But for individual believers and the church, its poison runs much deeper.

The Church's Syncretism with Secularism Has Locked Us Out of Reality

Secularism corrupted the church's morality much like idolatry corrupted Old Testament Israel. Theologians often divide the practice of a religion into the ethical/moral on the one hand and the cultic on the other. The moral requirements are encompassed in its commandments, while the cultic aspect relates to the ceremonial practices, or what we today usually mean by the term *worship*.

Remember Old Testament Israel and its syncretism. They continued the ceremonial worship of the LORD (sacrifices, washings, clean and unclean foods), but by adding the practices of idolatry, broke the moral commandments with the worship of graven images, cultic prostitution, and failure to observe the Sabbath. In the same way, the church today enthusiastically observes the cultic practices of Christianity (worship, singing, baptism, and communion) but violates the New Testament commandments with impunity. But as was true for Israel, even our most ardent worship is invalidated by our violation of God's commands. Recall Samuel's warning in 1 Samuel 15:23, "Has the LORD as much delight in burnt offerings and sacrifices as in obeying the voice of the LORD?" What the Old Testament idols did to Israel's worship, secularism has done to the church.

But the immorality of syncretism is more pernicious than simple disobedience because it involves not just a violation of a commandment but a redefinition of what is considered true. Recall a point from Chapter 2, "God, Knowledge and Morality," that morality constrains knowledge. That is, morality determines what is and isn't allowable within our truth system. Our morality influences our concepts and determines what is and isn't permissible to consider, creating a perimeter, much like the edge of a table. Any thought within the perimeter is allowable and fair game for contemplation on that moral table. If morality changes, then a new table is created, and new thoughts may be formed in accordance with the new table's perimeter.

God created the universe with an intrinsic morality that reflects His own righteous character. This is initially expressed in Genesis 1 with His repeated declarations that His creation is not morally neutral matter and energy, but good. Therefore, if we do not accept God's morality, we are no longer thinking about spiritual reality but a world of our own making. Rejecting biblical morality, we open the door to consideration of things that could not otherwise be considered within a Christian truth framework.

For example, the idea of marriage between homosexuals is unthinkable within a Christian moral framework. That doesn't mean someone within that framework cannot imagine such a possibility but rather that it is impossible to enact such a concept and still remain within the parameters of biblical morality.

But secular morality defines an entirely different truth system, transporting its adherents into an alternate conception of reality. Consider the secular concept of gender fluidity. In the Christian worldview, God determines an individual's sexual identity and its expression; but in the secular worldview, the individual determines for himself his gender and associated sexual expression. In the former, sexual identity is fixed and regulated by biblical commandments; in the latter, it is fluid and open to endless interpretation. Disagreeing with God about morality has profound implications for this life and the next.

Similarly, it is unthinkable to wed Christianity to Islam, Hinduism, or any other religion, for each articulates discrepant moralities and worldviews. Such commingling with another religion violates the commandment to serve but one God and causes us to give our souls to that which cannot save us. Yet this is what the church has done by syncretizing with secular ideologies.

But this brings us to an important and unique feature of the sin of syncretistic idolatry. The idolater not only breaks a commandment of his religion, but he also unwittingly imports portions of the worldview of another religion into his belief system. The Christian thief or adulterer violates the moral code of his religion, but he does not embrace an alien worldview.

Morality alone does not define what actions are permissible to consider but also the entire worldview of the religion. The idolater has both sinned (a moral violation) and accepted a worldview contrary to his native religion. When Christians accept the tenets of secularism, we both commit the sin of idolatry and accept its false worldview. Therefore, the sin of idolatry is doubly damning, opening the door for Christians to believe all manner of evil. The thief or adulterer may repent, but the idolater falls prey to the deceptive power of his newfound syncretism and cannot see his need to do so.

The delusion created by accepting secularism's temporal worldview bars the believer from true knowledge. Remember our discussion in Chapter 5, "The Church and Science," that both science and the Bible agree that a reality we cannot directly perceive underlies experience, but the Bible teaches that this underlying realm of causes is spiritual. To ignore this realm locks us out of reality and compromises our faculty of reason. This doesn't mean that idolatrous people can no longer balance their checkbooks or engage in science or other intellectual enterprises. Rather, idolatry impairs reason's ability to perform the purpose for which it was given—to know and love God! When reason is deployed for any other primary purpose, it leads to sin, error, pride, and presumption. Let's consider how this has played out for the modern church.

Secularism Influences How We Read and Interpret Scripture

Secularism's corrupting effect on reason can be seen in the church's reinterpretation of Scripture to accommodate its new false worldview. Paul writes in 2 Corinthians 5:10, "For we must all appear before the judgment seat of Christ, that each one may be recompensed for his deeds in the body, according to what he has done, whether good or bad."

This passage makes it impossible for Christians to follow the dictates of a morality that is based only on considerations of the present life. Yet the church today ignores the clear biblical teaching that believers are directly accountable to God.

How do we rationalize disregarding this? To embrace secularism, we must find a way to invalidate the above passage on judgment. The modern church has accomplished this by abusing the biblical doctrine of grace. Many in the church today preach that for all intents and purposes, grace obligates God to forgive all sin and to eliminate any and all eternal consequences or judgment for that sin.

If this is true, then Christ must either stare into an empty book when He judges me or whatever consequences might exist must be inconsequential. In this way, we use a doctrine of Scripture we like (grace) to eliminate a doctrine of Scripture that we do not like (judgment). We don't lose our ability to reason but rather our reasoning issues from a depraved mind (Romans 1:28).

God does not take kindly to using His Word in this way! Both grace and judgment are true. Grace does not eliminate the consequences for sin.

In Romans 14:10–12, Paul confirms that "we shall all stand before the judgment seat of God . . . [and] then each one of us shall give an account of himself to God." He warns in Galatians 6:7–8, "Do not be deceived, God is not mocked; for whatever a man sows, this he will also reap. For the one who sows to his own flesh shall from the flesh reap corruption, but the one who sows to the Spirit shall from the Spirit reap eternal life." He reiterates in 1 Corinthians 3:10–15 that each man should be careful how he builds on Christ's foundation, for he will either receive a reward or suffer loss for his work and be saved but "so as through fire."

By ignoring these unambiguous passages on eternal accountability for temporal behavior, we become guilty of the charge of Jude 4: "For certain persons have crept in unnoticed, those who were long beforehand marked out for this condemnation, ungodly persons who turn the grace of God into licentiousness and deny our only Master and Lord, Jesus Christ." Jude warns against using the grace of God as license to sin, but in our embrace of secularism, we have failed to heed this warning. Instead, secular morality and its worldview drive how we read the Scripture.

God's Authority Has Been Undermined

How we read the Scripture is of integral importance because it determines whether or not we are tethered to the underlying spiritual reality of the universe, which is grounded in the authority of God. Paul declares in 1 Corinthians 11:3, "But I want you to understand that Christ is the head of every man, and the man is the head of a woman, and God is the head of Christ."

This statement expresses the reality of the authority structure that God built into the universe and human relationships and is not a solicitation of our opinion on the subject. In this verse, we see how the authority within the Godhead extends to the human race and tethers us to the spiritual reality beyond our senses. A full explanation of this relationship is beyond the limits of this book, but I suggest that the relationship between Father and Son within the Trinity is the gold standard and model for all to follow.

In John 4:34, 5:30 and 6:38, Jesus declares that His mission is to subordinate Himself to the will of His Father. This is the heart of submission! And in the same way, men ought to subordinate their wills to their head, Jesus Christ. This concept is not complicated, but how many men, following the example of Christ, are obsessed with doing the will of Jesus Christ in their lives? And if we choke on this point, how many women are obsessed with seeking the will of their husbands? Both men and women resist this clear teaching with all their being, and not without reason, but with fallen, secular, human reason, which considers only the temporal.

We reason that since grace eliminates all consequences for sin, we need only be concerned with this present life, and so why should we make the sacrifice required to emulate Christ? The cost to obey is high (it costs us our wills), and the cost to disobey low (or so we believe). Being tethered to reality is the furthest thing from our minds.

Why does being tethered to reality, seeing things as they really are, matter? It matters because we were not made for the world as it now is, but for the world which is to come. We were made for "the city which has foundations, whose architect and builder is God" (Hebrews 11:10). For "our citizenship is in heaven" (Philippians 3:20), and God expects us to act like it! He is preparing us for that eternity by teaching us to abide with Him here on earth.

Central to that citizenship is the issue of authority. Who gets to define morality and knowledge/reality for us? God is the King of heaven and will one day visibly rule earth as well, and He expects to be Lord of our lives now.

In Matthew 8:5–13, Jesus marvels at the unparalleled faith of a centurion. When Jesus offers to come to his home to heal his servant, the centurion responds,

> Lord, I am not worthy for You to come under my roof, but just say the word, and my servant will be healed. For I, too, am a man under authority, with soldiers under me; and I say to this one,

"Go!" and he goes, and to another, "Come!" and he comes, and to my slave, "Do this!" and he does it."

What made this man so remarkable? He understood two things: 1) his own unworthiness; and 2) Jesus' authority. Humility and submission are inextricably linked: we see our unworthiness precisely because we understand that an authority exists who is greater than us, one whose expectations we have failed to meet. This humility directly contrasts the arrogance at the root of scientific materialism and secularism. Instead, we do well to emulate this man of whom Jesus marveled, "Truly I say to you, I have not found such great faith with anyone in Israel."

Authority cannot exist without fear. No child would consistently obey his parents unless they were capable of enforcing consequences for his behavior. The child must fear both his parents and the consequences of disobeying them for the parent to have meaningful authority over him.

But under the influence of secularism, the church believes that accountability for the Christian is either non-existent or inconsequential. Without judgment there is nothing to fear, and God and the Bible are no longer authoritative in any important way. We have become guilty of the indictment of Romans 3:18: "There is no fear of God before their eyes." We have lost the fear of the Lord that is the beginning of knowledge (Proverbs 1:7).

Rejecting the truth takes on a life of its own, resulting in an ever-increasing detachment from reality.

We Are Listening to the Dictates of Arrogant, Self-Interested Intellectuals

This leads us to the more immediate limitations of accepting a secular worldview. If God is no longer the authority on matters of morality, who then gets to define the two key concerns of secularism, "well-being" and "mankind"? First, who gets to define what "well-being" looks like—the Democrats, the Republicans, the Libertarians, the socialists, the European Union, Russia, China, or the Islamists—and what of the smaller factions, whose views are not represented by these groups? How should this be adjudicated, given the divergent opinions of these many factions?

At the risk of sounding conspiratorial, the answer is already emerging. There is a small intellectual class who simply "knows" and a much larger class of those who must obey. This intellectual class holds a secular/Marxist and scientifically materialist worldview and by their extreme brilliance of mind they instruct the rest of us. Anthony Daniels, in his introduction to *Last Exit to Utopia* by Jean-Francois Revel, summarizes:

> Intellectuals, the justification for whose existence is that they have a superior understanding of the world to that of non-intellectuals . . . not only

want to think well of themselves; but they want to be important. The attraction of ideology is that it offers a simple principle, or a few simple principles, by which to understand the world; and, of course, it offers the prospect of power to those who know and wield those principles with the greatest facilities. It seems to me likely that inside every Marxist Western intellectual there has been a Stalin trying to get out.[1]

By listening to the secularists, the church has traded the protection of a loving God for the dictates of the arrogant self-interested intellectual who opposes her very existence.

We Are Sacrificing Individuals for the "Good" Of Mankind

But even more dangerously, we have sacrificed the individual to the voracious demands of mankind. We do well to remember that mankind is an abstraction. Jesus Christ did not die for an abstraction—He died for individuals. Though God loves the world, *individuals* who believe, not *corporate* mankind, are the recipients of salvation (John 3:16). Through Christ's death, Christianity elevated the worth of the individual beyond anything the world had ever conceived. But when the good of mankind is the goal, the individual always suffers. Consider John 11:47–50:

Therefore the chief priests and the Pharisees convened a council, and were saying, "What are we doing? For this man is performing many signs. If we let Him go on like this, all men will believe in Him, and the Romans will come and take away both our place and our nation.'" But a certain one of them, Caiaphas, who was high priest that year, said to them, "You know nothing at all, nor do you take into account that it is expedient for you that one man should die for the people, and that the whole nation not perish."

The question at the center of this issue is whether the locus for justice lies with the individual or with the group. Christianity maintains it is the individual because the individual is made in the image and likeness of God regardless of ethnicity, sex, or social background, and is therefore of infinite importance, but also individually accountable for his behavior. The sovereign God of the Bible is capable of ensuring the good of mankind without sacrificing the good of the individual. He therefore expects His people to care for the individual (love one another and seek the salvation of souls) and leave the fate of humanity to Jesus Christ. Secularism, in holding that mankind, and not the individual, is the focal point, tramples on the interests of the individual in favor of the group. This principle is already at work in our courts and legislatures, and it is only the beginning of the increasingly virulent assault against Christians. When "the good of mankind" conflicts with the good of the individual, the individual always suffers.

The adoption of a secular worldview is finally a problem because it unleashes desire. Recall that the Enlightenment was committed to building a world on human reason and that secularism is the latest expression of that impulse. But is secularism really based on reason? Friedrich Nietzsche posited that no rational basis for morality exists. Though the question is beyond my reach, I suspect he was correct. As we've already established, morality depends on one's worldview, which in turn is a matter of faith. If one accepts the New Testament worldview that this life is preparation for an eternity with God, then biblical morality is the only rational response. But if the secularist is correct that morality is based solely on temporal considerations, then a different morality can be considered. But based on what? If Nietzsche is correct, then it is not based on reason. He supplied an answer, which he called the will to power. Naked will/desire rules over reason. But how can this be so?

Though we take great pride in our reason, it is in fact a very weak faculty. It cannot alone withstand the withering assault of its much stronger brother, desire. If you doubt this, close your eyes and think about what you want, and then close them again and think about what you need. Which of these two is more vivid? Or consider Solomon and all of his wisdom. Even the wisest man in history was incapable of resisting the seduction of his desires.

Reason had long been allied to Christianity to protect mankind from itself and its naked desire because reason could not stand alone. With the destruction of the Christian worldview and its attendant morality, desire now reigns supreme under a secular banner. And the church now flies this same banner. The secular Christian focuses on the here and now and lets God and the afterlife take care of themselves. What makes me happy now supplants what pleases God, both now and for all eternity. My will and desire now dictate the course of my life irrespective of the biblical commandments; obedience-optional Christianity becomes the norm.

We Have Elevated Temporal Comfort and Equity Over Salvation

Though there are many examples of how the church has become secular (including sexuality as previously discussed), church discipline and social justice stand out as two pertinent illustrations. The Bible clearly teaches the need to discipline the defiant, willfully sinning believer (Matthew 18:15–20; 1 Corinthians 5). The biblical reason to execute church discipline is to lead the sinner to repentance because the Bible sets a premium on that person's eternity and tells us that biblical love calls us to be motivated by this as well.

But the secular worldview, with its concern for the temporal, views this as unloving. Instead of conforming to the authority of God, the church today elevates the temporal comfort of the sinner (and those charged with confronting the sinner) above concern for his soul. Hence tolerance has replaced biblical love.

The church's increasing fascination with social justice follows the same principle of elevating temporal comfort and temporal equity over salvation. The church has long been a proponent of Christian charity, the meeting of people's temporal needs. But in the past, it has viewed this as a means to the end of sharing the gospel. Under the influence of secularism this is no longer the case.

My daughter recently attended a benefit concert for a Christian organization committed to ending child slavery. Though it was held at a church and both the organization and the musicians were Christians, the entire presentation not once mentioned sharing the gospel with children freed from slavery. The children were set free from bondage to men, but no mention was made of setting them free from bondage to sin and death. Jesus said, "For what shall it profit a man to gain the whole world, and forfeit his soul? For what shall a man give in exchange for his soul?" (Mark 8:36-37). Yet the secular church has no room for biblical love or the Great Commission—it is too busy seeking happiness in the here and now.

At this juncture it is worth remembering the words of Soren Kierkegaard, the nineteenth-century Danish philosopher, on the place of Christian scholarship. Kierkegaard deplored what modernity was doing to

the Bible and the church. Consider his words from
Provocations:

> The matter is quite simple. The Bible is very easy
> to understand. But we Christians are a bunch of
> scheming swindlers. We pretend to be unable
> to understand it because we know very well
> that the minute we understand, we are obliged
> to act accordingly. Take any words in the New
> Testament and forget everything except pledging
> yourself to act accordingly. My God, you will say,
> if I do that my whole life will be ruined. How
> would I ever get on in the world? Herein lies
> the real place of Christian scholarship. Christian
> scholarship is the Church's prodigious invention
> to defend itself against the Bible, to ensure that
> we can continue to be good Christians without
> the Bible coming too close. Oh, priceless
> scholarship, what would we do without you?
> Dreadful it is to fall into the hands of the living
> God. Yes, it is even dreadful to be alone with the
> New Testament.

These words were penned more than 150 years ago!
Yet they perfectly illustrate how the Christian scholarship
of today, with its predominantly secular worldview, has
been meticulously crafted to shield the believer from any
need to obey God's commandments unless we feel like

doing so. But Kierkegaard couldn't afford to hide behind "Christian scholarship," and neither can we.

It is hopefully apparent by now that for the Christian, scientific materialism, secularism, and cultural Marxism (to which we will turn next) are false idols, and cannot be legitimately embraced by Christ's followers. But these godless and humanistic worldviews are crueler and more a lie than even the pagan idolatry of antiquity. For as loathsome as that false worship was, it still contained a few vestiges of what is true and good. Those idolaters of yore knew what we have forgotten. They knew that a world existed beyond the senses, and that the gods, and not they themselves, were masters of human destiny. They understood that sacrifice to the divine was a central and necessary part of life. And they recognized that there was a wisdom higher than man's.

For all that was wrong with ancient idolatry, it bestowed on men the salutary blessing of humility. With all the "advances" of modernity, such is our lowly estate, the pagans knew more than we. And in forgetting these simplest and most basic truths, we blindly stumble toward a reckoning with a God who "is opposed to the proud, but gives grace to the humble" (James 4:6). Surely, the Day of Judgment will be more tolerable for them than for us.

We will now turn to cultural Marxism, the final pillar in the temple of the religion of man.

CHAPTER 7

The Church
and Cultural Marxism

CULTURAL MARXISM WAS the torpedo that sank modern institutional Christianity. Although it is popularly known by the innocuous "political correctness," it is not a benign or benevolent social agenda. Rather it is a well-crafted atheistic ideology whose avowed aim is to destroy Christianity and the Western culture Christianity helped to produce.

A small group of Marxist thinkers initially developed it in the 1920s and '30s as a strategy to enable Marxism to infiltrate and replace Western culture from the inside. From their posts in our universities and the media, it has gradually seeped into our culture and replaced the biblical worldview without most of us even being aware of its existence. As Michael Walsh describes in his book, *The Devil's Pleasure Palace,* it is waging "a culture war, a war which has been raging since the Garden of Eden that manifests itself today in the unceasing attack of cultural

Marxism (which molts and masquerades under many names, including liberalism, progressivism, social justice, environmentalism, anti-racism, etc.) upon what used to be called the Christian West."[1]

It has achieved a stranglehold on our culture because it perfectly completes the ideologies of science and secularism in that it provides a philosophical framework for achieving a man-made utopia. Thus its allure is the elusive promise of Eden and Babel that so appeals to our lust for autonomy—a perfectly just and equal utopia on earth defined by men and without any God to whom to answer. Unfortunately, although the utopia has not yet materialized, it has almost completed its avowed mission of destroying Christian culture, and by extension, the church.

Cultural Marxism views any form of traditional authority or morality as the chief barrier to realizing its aims, and its assault has been disastrous for the modern institutional church in three important ways:

1. Its promotion of sexual permissiveness has resulted in the proliferation of extramarital sexual activity, homosexuality, and divorce, thereby eviscerating Christian morality.
2. It has destroyed the authority of men to head their homes, demolishing the Christian nuclear family, and denigrating men in general by undermining masculinity and marginalizing men in society.

3. It has weakened the authority of the Bible and led to selective obedience of the Scripture at the discretion of the believer.

This assault on the authority of Scripture has replaced reason—the necessary human faculty for apprehending Scripture—with feeling, emotion and desire.

This, in turn, has effectively destroyed God's ability to define knowledge and morality for His people, and the church has become man-centered rather than God-centered.

The Ideological Foundation of Marxism Feeds Man's Sinful Nature

Before we discuss the history of cultural Marxism and how it has devastated the church, we must first explain how its ideas have so enchanted and ensnared the West.

Though the West won the political and economic Cold War with communism, in a horrible twist of irony, it was Marxism that destroyed the Western soul. Nikolaus Lobkowicz, a former professor of philosophy at the University of Notre Dame and expert on world communism, chronicles this in his 1985 paper, "Marxism as the Ideology of Our Age." He argues that Marxism expresses an idea that strikes a resonant chord in the hearts of sinful men, and this idea has come to dominate our worldview. He writes,

The spread of Marxism in the late '60s and early '70s was like the outburst of a new world wide religion . . . Marxism must have sparked a hidden longing of the Western world. It must have been the obvious answer to—indeed, the synthesis of—what many if not most of its intellectuals believed in (pp. 2–3).[2]

Though many Westerners view Marxism as a set of social and economic ideas associated with now-bankrupt totalitarian regimes, the ideology of cultural Marxism is not merely social and economic. Instead we find ourselves struggling against an overarching worldview of godless autonomy informed by the two wicked ideas from the temptation in the Garden: 1) God's not good; and 2) You can replace Him.

Marxism, of course, simplifies the endeavor by denying the existence of God altogether. In doing so, enlightened man is empowered to define for himself what constitutes truth, morality, and even the reality that defines our circumstances. Marxism offers what the ideologies of science and secularism long needed to complete their aims—the systemic framework to accomplish this emancipation. In short, Marxism offers what Lobkowicz identifies as the "secular redemption of man" without God (p. 8).

For our purposes, I want to focus on two pairs of ideas that Lobkowicz identifies which will help us to understand how Marxist ideology has permeated our thinking. These ideas may not seem either appealing or familiar, but they help to explain the underlying backbone of Marxism that evolved into cultural Marxism. In these ideas we see the seeds of the attack on absolute morality and authority (including scriptural authority) and the replacement of these forces by desire.

As I outline these ideas, ask yourself, "What is the basis for believing this; by whose authority is this said to be true; and why should I accept this?"

The first pair of ideas concerns the Marxist conception of man and history. Marxism denies the existence of God, and thus the Marxist ideology revolves around the idea that man must provide for himself—there is no loving God to do so. Further, man is only a biologic creature, being soulless like the animals. But humans differ from the animals in two important ways: 1) Man is rational; and 2) In humans, the satisfaction of one biologic need causes new needs to emerge, a process necessary for generating human progress.

Therefore, according to Marx, man evolved by purely natural means into a rational being, a belief that was bolstered by the theory of evolution, which arose concurrently. History became meaningful because, and only because, humans became rational creatures. As Lobkowicz explains, "due to the emergence of man, matter has generated meaning, for with man history came about, and history has a direction" (p. 4). Thus meaning for the

Marxist derives solely from the rationality of man rather than the divine purposes of God.

Because of man's reason, history came to have purpose. But Marx wanted more. History must also progress on an ever upward trajectory. To achieve this, Marx turned to the second unique biological feature of man mentioned previously.

When an animal's need for food is met, it does not develop a new and different need; it still only wants food. But man is different. When his need for food is met, he continues to want food, but he also develops new and different needs. Now he wants to build a house. But having built his house, he wants not just a mate but love. And even that is not enough, for having found love, he now wants self-esteem and self-actualization. The satisfaction of one need leads to the development of another (think of psychologist Abraham Maslow's Hierarchy of Needs, which is quintessentially Marxist anthropology, expounded in his 1943 paper, "A Theory of Human Motivation"). The pinnacle of the pyramid in Maslow's hierarchy is self-actualization, the Marxist goal for man.

In these two ways, Marx claimed, history not only came to have meaning, but also a necessarily upward trajectory—which is to say, history is progress. Individual people are not important, but man as a species is transformed by that upward trajectory.

If Marx is right, that progress results from the satisfaction of man's new and emerging needs, then what is the source of these new needs? According to Maslow, we achieve self-actualization (the highest need in humans) by acting on our passions and desires. Marx furthered this by saying that as each of us surrenders to our own passions and desires, the entire species will be uplifted. Desire replaces reason and revelation as our guiding light, and we become like the animals that Marx and Darwin believed us to be.

But even this was not enough for Marx; he wanted to redefine truth as well. He did so by linking a second pair of ideas: progress/truth.

For him, progress is further defined by two criteria: 1) mastery over the universe, and 2) emancipation from our "dire past." To the Marxist, the past is always by default dire because it subsists on a lower rung of the evolutionary pyramid. It must be dire because it was in the past, and only the future can be positive.

Whatever contributes to one or both of these goals is by definition "truth." As Lobkowicz notes, "[Whenever] a claim, a theory, or a philosophy contributes to man's mastery over the universe and to his emancipation from his dire past, it is true; if it does not contribute to it, it is false, no matter how empirical, scientific or lofty it may be" (p. 9). Therefore, there is no absolute or objective truth, only a functional truth that promotes the "betterment" of the species.

Science is the natural partner of Marxism because it, too, is largely concerned with achieving mastery over nature. Even environmentalism is a child of this belief, because it seeks to master nature as well, just in a different way.

But who will emancipate us from the "dire" past and who says that it is dire? The answer to both questions is an elite intellectual class who sees the world in the Marxist way. They call for emancipation from our dire past through the same means that Marx did: "by relentless criticism of all existing conditions" (*Writings of the Young Marx on Philosophy and Society*, 1843, p. 212). Marx aspired to emulate the Devil's sentiment in the German legend of Faust, that "everything that exists deserves to perish."[3]

This elite class of "those who know" has replaced God, redefining truth, but doing so in a negative way, by tearing down existing structures of authority and morality to make room for the "progress" of humanity. This new authority is not reason or revelation, but desire. In this, we see the germ of the idea that traditional male authority, scriptural authority, and biblical morality are relics of the past from which we must be freed.

Before discussing how these ideas have ravaged the church, review in your mind the highly speculative nature of all that was just written! Why would anyone embrace such thinking, especially in a largely Christian culture like the West? Everything in this ideology is antithetical to Christianity and the Bible! Like Lobkowicz, I fear we have accepted these ideas because they find deep resonance in our rebellious hearts. At the end of this chapter, we will return to this important question.

The Birth of Cultural Marxism Began After Traditional Marxism

Though traditional Marxism appealed to many intellectuals, it did not initially gain widespread acceptance in the West; Christianity ensured that the masses would not accept it. But what if Christianity could be destroyed or at least neutered? This was the task that the cultural Marxists set for themselves.

Cultural Marxism's intellectual history began well before it became popularly known as political correctness. Its roots are found in the period around and shortly after World War I, and its original theorists were the Hungarian communist Georg Lukacs and the Italian communist Antonio Gramsci, who recognized a need to modify Marx's theory of communism. (This history is chronicled in numerous sources, including "The Origins of Political Correctness" by Bill Lind,[4] "What Is the Frankfurt School?" by Dr. Gerald L. Akinson,[5] and "Deconstructing President Obama's Stance on Israel" by Bill Flax.[6])

Communism, as articulated by Marx, was a social and economic theory, whereas that of Lukacs and Gramsci was also a cultural theory. Why the change?

The revision was necessary because Marx's original theory collided with history and was found wanting. He made at least three predictions which were refuted by historical events. First, he predicted that the Communist Revolution would occur in the most industrialized and capitalistic countries. Instead, it occurred in 1917 in Russia, the least developed of the European countries. Secondly, he predicted that when any sort of war broke out, the workers of the belligerent countries would not fight for their countries but would instead unite across national lines behind a workers' revolution. Instead, when World War I began, they fought patriotically for their countries. Thirdly, he posited that when the Revolution did begin, the workers would enthusiastically support it. Once again, the Russian peasants did not conform to his theory, and the Revolution was instigated and championed largely by idealistic intellectuals.

To explain these evident failures, Lukacs and Gramsci reasoned that Marx had not sufficiently taken into account culture's impact on the people; accordingly, their brand of Marxism has been dubbed "cultural Marxism." In effect, they argued that the culture had rendered people in general, but the workers in particular, too stupid to recognize where their best interest lay. And that culture which blinded them was Christian.

So Christian culture, with its values and institutions and its constricting definition of truth and morality, needed to be destroyed. Lukacs theorized "that the great obstacle to the creation of a Marxist paradise was the culture: Western civilization itself ... . 'Who will save us from Western Civilization?'"[7]

This culturally revisionist reworking of Marx coalesced into what became known as the Frankfurt School, after its 1923 birthplace, Frankfurt, Germany. It was inspired by the Marx-Engels-Lenin Institute in Moscow and was originally called the Institute for Social Research.

But by 1933, Hitler had risen to power in Germany, and the members of the Frankfurt School, who were overwhelmingly Jewish, fled to the United States. They took up residence at our universities, including Columbia, Brandeis, and the University of California at Berkeley, among others, and eventually in Hollywood, believing, as Gramsci posited, that the new carriers of the revolution would be the intellectuals instead of the proletariat. Members included Theodor Adorno, Max Horkheimer, Herbert Marcuse and Erich Fromm. Other figures who later became associated with them were Jurgen Habermas, Walter Benjamin and Abraham Maslow.

The Weapon of Cultural Marxism: Systematized Criticism

Critical theory was the brainchild of their new movement, a theory described by Horkheimer in 1937 as the "means to liberate human beings from the circumstances that enslave them." Consistent with its name, its chief weapon for destroying the current culture was constant and relentless criticism. Michael Walsh characterized it as a "guerrilla assault on Western and American culture which holds that there is no received tenet of civilization that should not be questioned or attacked."[8] As Walsh relates, it directed "an unremitting assault on Western values and institutions, including Christianity, the family, conventional sexual morality, national patriotism, and adherence in general to any institution or set of beliefs that blocked the path to revolution."[9] Bill Lind observes that the theory uses "the most destructive criticism possible, designed to bring the current order down."[10]

One of its most successful arguments has been to point out hypocrisy: it contrasts the present reality of Western culture and its beliefs with Western culture's ideals in order to deride and delegitimize it. (Of course, it fails to recognize that none of us, including the proponents of critical theory, live up to our own standards.) As Bill Flax encapsulates it, "Derision was their weapon, language and arts their hunting ground and Western Civilization their prey."[10]

Because critical theory systematizes criticism, it necessarily systematizes ingratitude and rebellion. Change is always good, present circumstances and authority always bad. In contrast, the Bible warns us in the very first verse of the Psalms not to "sit in the seat of scoffers," and in Proverbs 24:21 to "fear the LORD and the king; do not associate with those who are given to change." Change may be good and fitting in many settings, but from the biblical perspective, no moral or spiritual improvement can be made upon the New Testament. All of the Old Testament led up to Christ, and now we look back at Him as the perfect, unchanging standard of God's truth with which we dare not tamper. This standard is precisely what the cultural Marxists have sought to destroy.

Herbert Marcuse was integral in embedding critical theory into the elite universities. He introduced the concept of "repressive tolerance," which he defined as "intolerance against movements from the Right and toleration of movements from the Left."[11] Again, my concern is not political but rather that repressive tolerance defines an entirely new morality and truth system in its intolerance for the speech of anyone opposed to the Left.

This concept was part of Marxism from the beginning, reflected in the origin of the term "political correctness," which was first used by Trotsky to describe the constantly changing "correct" modes of Soviet political thought.[12] In this way, by being intolerant of the speech used by groups opposed to the Left, not only is the discussion of those ideas suppressed, but the thoughts behind them as well.

Words define truth and alter our thinking; altering our thinking in turn molds our souls (Romans 12:2). The Bible tells us that believers are born of the Word of God, and therefore our minds must be nourished by it (1 Peter 1:23, 2:2). Under the influence of repressive tolerance, the church has conformed to the lies of cultural Marxism rather than being transformed by the Word of God. Changing our language has changed who we are.

The Captivation of the West: Deception, Rebellion and Eroticism

The Frankfurt School used a carrot-and-stick technique to sell its agenda to the West. We see this clearly in the titles of two of its most influential works, *The Authoritarian Personality*, published by Theodor Adorno and several other Frankfurt school members in 1950, and *Eros and Civilization: A Philosophical Inquiry into Freud*, published by Herbert Marcuse in 1955.

The Authoritarian Personality articulates the stick portion of their strategy, which included expunging the "authoritarian personality" by attacking the patriarchal family and the masculine gender.[13] *Eros and Civilization* depicts the carrot, which deployed eroticism to destroy the existing moral order. Marcuse referred to this new sexual permissiveness as "polymorphous perversity."[14]

Their critique of Western culture oddly blended Marx with Freud and targeted both Christianity and the Enlightenment. Possibly because it was less threatening to attack the Enlightenment than to direct a frontal assault on Christianity, their enterprise began there. The Enlightenment figures had three things in common—they were all white, male, and educated (reason was their guide). Therefore, whiteness, maleness (particularly male authority), and reason became the focus of their criticism.

The attack on whiteness was part of the stick used to force the West to swallow its lies. In a genius move, they accurately observed and emphasized the gross mistreatment of black and other ethnic minorities by whites. Based on the Golden Rule, nobody could deny or justify the horrors of slavery, Jim Crow laws, or segregation. The cultural Marxists used the truth of these historical abuses by whites to argue for the complete destruction of Western culture and its morality. Like Satan before them, they wove a truth into the fabric of the lie. And believe the lies we did.

Men were the second target of their stick strategy, an attack made successful by allying it with the carrot of sexual permissiveness. Men to be sure had mistreated women, but this was not their point. Rather, they argued that there was something inherently wrong with maleness. Maleness, in their critique, was the epitome of the "authoritarian personality," and as such should be suppressed and, if possible, eliminated. Not only so, but sexual differences were "socially learned constructs" not intrinsic to either sex, and for humanity to progress, we should move to what Abraham Maslow called a more "general humanness" rather than defined sexual roles that culture had imposed on us.[15]

To many at the time, this seemed like intellectual babble. But the members of the Frankfurt School were not fools, and they turned to Freud for assistance. Freud had argued that much of what was wrong with Western civilization could be attributed to pent-up sexual repression. The Frankfurt School incorporated this idea into their strategy to break down the sexual norms and morality of the West, advocating both heterosexual and homosexual sexual permissiveness. The coincident rise of feminism embraced this agenda as part of its goal of giving women all the opportunities that men enjoyed, including the right to sexual liaisons without commitment.

This was the Holy Grail for libidinous men from time immemorial and the spoonful of sugar that enticed them to swallow the medicine of women competing with them (and eventually overtaking them) in academics, the marketplace, and the home. To say this another way, Western civilization, and later the church, sold its soul for a one-night stand. Women lost their virtue, and men their honor and authority.

The third focus of the Frankfurt School was an attack on reason. As we have mentioned, one of the central tenets of Marxism is that the satisfaction of one's material needs is the only truly important force in history. There is no god, nor absolute truth or morality; only the satisfaction of our biological/material needs. Again, according to Marx, meeting these needs, by definition, results in Progress, and Progress is defined as that which contributes to our mastery of the universe and emancipates us from the dire past.

In this bizarre system, truth is by definition partial, not rationally understood, and determined only by what we desire for ourselves. But reason cannot function without a foundation on which to operate. As I have argued before, reason is too weak a faculty to withstand alone the powerful force of desire. Without the anchor of absolute, transcendent truth, reason is supplanted by desire and emotions.

To demonstrate how cultural Marxism appeals to our desires, not our reason, let's consider a Marxist hypothesis: whatever emancipates us from our dire past is by definition true. First, ask yourself, "Is that a rational and factual evaluation, or is it something we just want/will/desire to be true?" Our "dire past" valued authority and was patriarchal. If the Marxist hypothesis is true, authority should be despised and men should be degraded and women elevated.

But is this conclusion based on reason or on desire? In the Garden of Eden, God created man and commanded him not to eat of the Tree of the Knowledge of Good and Evil. He then placed him in authority over the animals and created Eve, who must have learned they should not eat of the Tree from Adam. Yet their disobedience inverted this order, Eve listening to an animal rather than her husband and Adam listening to his wife rather than God. The events of the Garden indicate that we have always longed to topple God's authority structure. It is our desire for rebellion, not our reason, to which Marxism appeals.

Or consider sexuality. In the past, our culture prized monogamous heterosexual relationships within the confines of marriage. Emancipation from our dire past would then entail advocating heterosexual extramarital, non-monogamous, and homosexual expressions of sexuality. Again, is this promotion derived from reason, or is it simply what we want? Of course, I (and Romans 1) argue that sexual indulgence has always appealed to us.

Cultural Marxism's Captivation of the United States Was Fueled by the Vietnam War

The student-led outrage over the Vietnam War in the 1960s and early '70s was the match that ignited the tinderbox of these ideas which the Frankfurt School had so carefully prepared. The young radicals had imbibed these ideas from their culturally Marxist professors, and in their view, the war was all the proof they needed that their teachers had been right all along.

Americans were weary of war. The enlightened and Christian West had already fought two world wars and a large regional conflict in Korea in that century alone. Now the government was embarking on yet another in Vietnam and enforcing an unpopular draft to fight it.

The cultural Marxists fomented this discontent by envisioning the Ho Chi Minh-led communist peasants as the tragic heroes of a misbegotten conflict. It was these rebels who bore the seeds of progress for a hopelessly lost Western world. As David Horowitz, one of the original Marxist student leaders at Berkeley, chronicles in his autobiography *Radical Son*, the radical student leadership believed this narrative and was determined to educate and coerce an initially reluctant American society to accept it as reality. Horowitz relates of his years at Berkeley, "We made our decisions collectively, and had a religious fervor toward the positions we took and the slogans that defined them[,] . . . slogans [that were] designed to consolidate majorities, but also to achieve agendas that would never have been defended by most people who eventually supported them."[16]

This generation of Baby Boomers believed its destiny was to transform the world into a Marxist utopia. Its rallying cries were inspired by Marcuse's *Eros and Civilization*, which arrived on campuses just in time to stoke the fire, and promoted the messages behind the famous slogans, "make love not war" and "if it feels good, do it." Resistance was modest and ineffective, particularly among the young, and the poison spread to all corners of America and Europe, and unfortunately, to the church.

Cultural Marxism Spread to the Church Through a "Christian" Revival

Ironically, its spread to the church was partially facilitated by a Christian revival among the young hippies, who became known as the Jesus People. They flocked to existing churches and started new ones, bringing their Marxism with them. Since then, these ideas have continued to leach into the church through the culture. The first effect of this was to break down the traditionally understood role of the sexes. Women began assuming leadership roles in the church, and men retreated from their headship role in their homes.

To most of us, raised in a post-culturally Marxist milieu, the reversal of the role of the sexes may seem irrelevant or even perhaps progressive. But recall our discussion in the last chapter, that in 1 Corinthians 11:3, God delineates the authority structure of the universe: God→ Christ→man→woman (the animals, though not mentioned in this passage, are under man's authority according to Genesis). Recall also that this authority structure is a not matter of our opinion or a cultural construct but is rather a dictate of the God who created the universe.

This authority structure was first attacked in the Garden by the serpent, when Eve chose to listen to an animal rather than her husband, and Adam chose to listen to his wife rather than God. But it has now been attacked on a global scale in these latter times. The accompanying chart illustrates this decomposition.

Figure 2: Challenges to the Authority Structure of God

The link between God and Christ was tested in the wilderness by the Devil, and was found to be secure (Matthew 4:8–10). But the link between man and Christ was tested and successfully severed by the Enlightenment, when man began to adopt his own reason rather than Christ's revelation as his authority. Now cultural Marxism's attack on male authority has fulfilled its self-proclaimed destiny by severing woman from man.

This disintegration of biblical authority has been coupled with a predictable descent into immorality. Because we are severed from Christ, He no longer defines morality for us. Though the church has lagged behind the culture in this, by casting a blind eye to its parishioners' new values, it eventually has come to tolerate, if not embrace, a sexual morality barely, if at all, different from that of the secular world.

But this new influx of Marxist ideas that swept in with the Jesus People and the influence of the outside culture introduced another dangerous idea as well. The student revolt of the '60s convinced the demonstrators that they could defy authority and get away with it. Although I am not at all sure that what followed was deliberate or conscious on the part of the Jesus People and other groups, they carried this lesson into their reading of Scripture. In their embrace of the doctrine of grace, they came to believe that grace eliminated all consequences of sin, a position that is well shy of orthodox.

As we discussed in the last chapter, in order to accept this reading, some troublesome scriptures to the contrary had to be ignored. Additional verses that speak to this issue include passages such as Matthew 16:27, Romans 2:16, Romans 14:10–12, and 2 Corinthians 5:10. This was the beginning of the church using Scripture to refute Scripture, and it has since honed this craft well. This abuse of grace has become the Christian version of repressive tolerance: we will tolerate immorality, but we will not tolerate teachings on authority or "restrictive" morality.

As a result, the church has embraced emotional subjectivism driven by desire and not reason. This is manifested by an emphasis on experiential worship and grace at the expense of understanding the Bible and obedience to its commandments. We go to church to feel good about ourselves and to be affirmed rather than challenged to become disciples who apply the Word in order to "enter by the narrow gate" (Matthew 7:13).

In summary, we see that cultural Marxism/political correctness has wrought devastating effects on the church. These include: 1) demolishing the biblically defined role of the sexes; 2) obliterating biblical morality, resulting in sexual permissiveness; and 3) devaluing reason's role in understanding the faith, resulting in widespread biblical illiteracy and emotionalism, emphasizing "feel-good" worship rather than conviction of sin and a call to repentance. Taken together, these effects have produced a homogenization of behavior and focus between the church and secular culture.

The net result has been that the church has become essentially secular in its worldview, shifting from an eternal focus on the soul and holiness to a temporal focus on fleshly self-gratification and happiness. In so doing, the church has lost its moral standing in society and is no longer a viable witness to a lost and dying world.

The Appeal of Cultural Marxism for the Church

Finally, the question remains as to why the poisonous ideas of Marxism were embraced by the church with so little resistance. We have hinted at this but now I would like to offer five reasons.

First, Marxist thinking placed man at the center, which is the rightful place according to sinful man. Former communist Whittaker Chambers observes in *Witness* that Marxism is "the vision of man's mind displacing God as the creative intelligence of the world . . . the promise whispered in the first days of creation under the tree of the knowledge of good and evil: 'ye shall be as gods'."[17] Christians have been all too enthusiastic in accepting this heresy because, despite the fact that Scripture refutes it, we believe it in the depths of our souls. It is our core belief that, if not Man with a capital *M*, then at least *I* should be the center of the universe.

Secondly, because we believe this, Marx's emphasis on emancipation captures our hearts. We view freedom as one of our most cherished rights, and Marx promises to set us free from all the strictures of our dire, dark and foolish past. But only Christ can truly free us, although the freedom He offers is from sin (John 8:32–36). Marx offers slavery to sin, Christ freedom from it, and deceived like Eve in the Garden, we chose slavery believing it to be freedom.

Thirdly, it frees us from accountability to apostolic authority. By portraying the past as dire, Marx has cut us off from that past. We see this everywhere, including in the curricula of our schools, which no longer teach the history of Western civilization. But for the believer, we have lost a far more important past—the past of the apostles. We view them through Marxist eyes instead of the biblical reality that they are the foundation of the church. Unconsciously deeming them a part of our dire past, we reject their teachings and commandments, labeling them as cultural commandments (and therefore not obligatory to the more "enlightened" people of today), and listen instead to the voice of our modern false teachers.

Fourthly, it enables us to follow our own desires. Truth is now relative and subjective rather than eternal and objective. If it doesn't "speak to me," I am not obligated by it, and this affirms my autonomy. I can pick and choose according to my own whims.

Finally, progress is all around us, leading us to believe that we know more than any who have preceded us. Our knowledge focuses on nature, which is the object of scientific inquiry. But what of knowledge of the soul and the spiritual? We have forgotten the hard work necessary for the only progress that truly matters—the progress of the soul. After all, it's easier to make an informed decision about our next smart phones than to examine the darkness of our souls and expose them to the Light that has come into the world. It's easier to indulge our appetites than to live the life of self-denial whereby our souls may become knit to our Redeemer.

In short, Marx gives us what we want; Christ offers what we need. And we have made our choice. We will turn next to the only solution open for the redemption of God's people from these secular ideologies: to return to an apostolic understanding of the Bible.

CHAPTER 8

The Importance of
the Apostles

HOW, IN A time-bound world of constant change, do you keep a timeless religion unchanged? That is the question that lies at the heart of this book. The ideologies we have elaborated, with their idolization of change and progress, have led the church to believe that preservation is unnecessary. Instead, the church, like our culture, is convinced that we can become more enlightened than our predecessors.

But "Jesus Christ is the same yesterday and today, yes and forever" (Hebrews 13:8). To evolve with the times means to depart from Christ. To the degree that the preceding chapters render an accurate picture of non-Christian Western thought's influence on the church, we have protected our timeless religion very poorly.

The church is highly market conscious and responds to the desires of its constituents. We as individual believers are the church, and each of us bears some blame. We must not only repent, but also find a way out. The way out is the subject of this chapter.

In Revelation 21:10–14, John describes the advent of the New Jerusalem at the end of the age:

> And [the angel] carried me away in the Spirit to a great and high mountain, and showed me the holy city, Jerusalem, coming down out of heaven from God, having the glory of God. Her brilliance was like a very costly stone, as a stone of crystal-clear jasper. It had a great and high wall, with twelve gates, and at the gates twelve angels; and names were written on them, which are the names of the twelve tribes of the sons of Israel. There were three gates on the east and three gates on the north and three gates on the south and three gates on the west. And the wall of the city had twelve foundation stones, and on them were the twelve names of the twelve apostles of the Lamb.

John's prophecy highlights the centrality of the apostles. Their teachings were not merely a springboard for church history; they are the immovable foundation stones of a church fixed in eternity.

Accordingly, the apostles, and the gospels and epistles that the Holy Spirit inspired them to write, must be the sole hermeneutic, or lens, through which the Bible must be read and understood by His people. Their beliefs and adherence to the biblical commandments must be our beliefs and adherence to the biblical commandments. Only by rooting ourselves to this bedrock can we withstand the assault of the secular ideas we have just discussed.

The New Testament Is Fixed Rather Than an Evolving Source of Truth

Remember that among the many differences between the Old Testament and the New is the element of time. The Old Testament spans many centuries and generations. Not only so but God works differently from the time of Adam to the prophets. From Abraham He raises up the nation of Israel, and through Moses gives them His law. They begin as a theocracy, later to be ruled by judges and finally by kings. Ultimately God sends them into exile to bring about repentance. All of this prepared the nation for His Son and served as a shadow of the heavenly things to be revealed in Christ (Hebrews 10:1).

This process occurred over centuries and involved many generations. But the New Testament is different. It spans only one generation—the generation of Jesus Christ and His apostles. We tend to read the New Testament through an Old Testament grid. That is, we erroneously believe that the history of the church parallels the history of Israel, and that the church, like Israel, should evolve over time.

This is nonsense. The Old Testament was an incremental revelation over a long period of time because it culminated with the revelation of Jesus Christ, who is the "consummation of the ages" and the "Word [Who] became flesh, and dwelt among us" (Hebrews 9:26; John 1:14). In that one generation who "beheld His glory" (John 1:14), God gave to Christ's church all the spiritual capital that she would need until His return. "For Christ is the end of the law for righteousness to everyone who believes" (Romans 10:4).

This doesn't mean nothing of value was added to the Christian corpus after the New Testament was written and canonized. Rather, any additional insights have value only to the degree to which they derive from and do not modify the gospels and epistles. For the biblical Christian, the Old Testament is a unity with the New and should be understood from the perspective of Christ's and the apostle's teachings. To the degree to which our new ideas deviate, they lead the church astray.

This begs the question as to why Christ gave the epistles to His church. Weren't the gospels sufficient? What do the epistles add? I posit that God gave them to freeze the timeless Christ in time. Relating to a timeless Christ requires clear and timeless eyes, and the apostles serve as our eyes. When we see Christ through the modern ideologies, we do so through the diseased and distorted, 2000-year-old cataracts of time and change.

The Epistles Are Essential to Preserving the Apostle's View of Christ

So how in a time-bound world of constant change *do* we keep a timeless religion unchanged?

The importance of this question lies in the observable fact that Christ can be and has been wedded to anything. To the capitalist Jesus was a capitalist, to the socialist a socialist, and to the crusader for social justice He was a social justice crusader. But He is none of these. He is the timeless and eternal Son of God.

Jesus appears so malleable to some because by themselves, the gospels are insufficient to cement the complete, eternal character of Christ. The gospels are largely narrative interspersed by Jesus' teachings, which were frequently given through parables. The epistles serve to explicate the narrative and Jesus' words. Prior to His death, He promised His disciples, "I have many more things to say to you, but you cannot bear them now. But when He, the Spirit of truth comes, He will guide you into all the truth; for He will not speak on His own initiative, but whatever He hears, He will speak" (John 16:12–13).

The writings of the apostles are intended to freeze Christ in time, allowing the church to see Him as they saw Him. The world changes, but Christ does not. And though the church may rebelliously evolve with the times, the faithful follower of Christ must resist being molded by the world or the changing church. This resistance requires having the mind of Christ, and understanding how to obtain His mind is therefore important.

Paul describes how the Holy Spirit gave the very words of God to the apostles:

> Yet we do speak wisdom among those who are mature; a wisdom, however, not of this age, nor of the rulers of this age, who are passing away; but we speak God's wisdom in a mystery, the hidden wisdom, which God predestined before the ages to our glory. . . . Now we have received, not the spirit of this world, but the Spirit who is from God, that we might know the things freely given to us by God, which things we also speak, not in words taught by human wisdom, but in those taught by the Spirit combining spiritual thoughts with spiritual words (1 Corinthians 2:6–7, 12–13).

He concludes his description with the statement, "But we have the mind of Christ" (verse 16). The "we" and "us" in the passage refers to the apostles and not to the Corinthians or anyone else. Instead, Paul refers to the Corinthians as "you" in 2:1–5 and again in chapter three and juxtaposes them with the apostles ("we"): the apostles "speak wisdom among the mature" (2:6), but the Corinthians could not receive it because they are "men of flesh, . . . babes in Christ" (3:1).

If all believers have the mind of Christ, why do we need Paul or the Bible? Recall that at conversion, the believer receives the Holy Spirit (Acts 2:38), but the mind of Christ is not immediately promised. Having the Holy Spirit and having the mind of Christ are not equivalent. Having the Holy Spirit is necessary to having the mind of Christ, but it is not sufficient. This distinction is critical because it demonstrates that Paul is arguing that he and the other apostles have the mind of Christ, not all believers. If we did have the mind of Christ, we would not have believed these ruinous ideologies.

The Holy Spirit is a gift; the mind of Christ must be acquired. Paul acquired the mind of Christ during his three years in Arabia with the risen Christ: "For I neither received it from men, nor was I taught it, but I received it through a revelation of Jesus Christ" (Galatians 1:12).

The apostles' experiences with Christ were unique. How then do we today gain His mind? Like the Corinthians and Galatians, you and I have the "mind of Christ" only to the degree that we have the mind of the apostles. By knowing, understanding, and applying their writings we come to have the mind of Christ. But this is a process and is not instantaneous, unlike the indwelling of the Holy Spirit at salvation. Furthermore, it is the reason for the command of Romans 12:2 that we "be transformed by the renewing of [our] mind[s]." Renewing our minds entails changing how we think. All permanent changes begin in the mind. And it is His mind that we seek, not our own or that of the world. This process may be incremental, but it is life-changing.

Christ does not change His mind when the world or the church changes its mind. Our minds must be conformed to His rather than the other way around. The apostles are the hermeneutic or filter through which we understand Christ. To be faithful to Christ is to believe and practice what the apostles believed and practiced with respect to the Word of God.

We Are Constrained to Abide in the Apostles' Teachings and Practices

In Revelation 2:1–7, Christ commends the Ephesian church for accurately identifying true versus false apostles. We are the beneficiaries of that work. But He chides them for leaving their "first love."

What this looked like is speculation. I suggest that "first love" refers to the beliefs and practices of the apostles. In John 15:9–10, Jesus commands His apostles: "Just as the Father has loved Me, I have also loved you; abide in My love. If you keep My commandments, you will abide in My love; just as I have kept My Father's commandments and abide in His love." We see here that Christ asks His apostles not to stray from His love, and that abiding in His love requires obedience to His commandments.

But whose understanding of His commandments are we to embrace? As we have seen in the preceding chapters, they can be easily reinterpreted to suit the times. John is again our source for the answer to this question. In 1 John 2:24, he says, "As for you, let that abide in you which you heard from the beginning. If what you heard from the beginning abides in you, you also will abide in the Son and in the Father."

John offers here a test for determining whether or not we abide in Christ. We abide in Him if "what [we] heard from the beginning abides in [us]." The beginning to which John is referring is Christ and His encounter with the apostles. Christ's investment of His truth in the disciples during His earthly ministry and in the apostle Paul following His resurrection forms the foundation of the church. This and only this view of Christ is eternal. "What was from the beginning, what we have heard, what we have seen with our eyes, what we beheld and our hands handled, concerning the Word of Life" is the eternal truth of Christ as witnessed by the apostles that John insists his listeners abide in (1 John 1:1). In other words, he says, believe and do what we apostles, who witnessed the Lord first hand, believed and did.

This is clearer when we think of ancient Israel and ask, *Who stood closer to God's truth as expressed in the Old Testament, Abraham and Moses on the one hand, or the Pharisees of Jesus' day on the other?* The question answers itself. So, then, does the follow-up question: *Who stands closer to God's truth as expressed in the New Testament, the apostles or the church today?*

John makes the same point again in 1 John 4:6,

We are from God; he who knows Gods listens to us; he who is not from God does not listen to us. By this we know the spirit of truth and the spirit of error.

This test of truth and error can only be answered by determining who the "we" and "us" are in the verse. Christians have never agreed with one another, so it cannot refer to believers in general. Otherwise the "we" becomes completely subjective, including whomever you wish it to be, and "the spirit of truth and error" would be fragmented beyond repair. I suggest the only plausible answer is to return to the "we" of chapter 1, verses 1 through 4—the apostles. The "spirit of truth," then, entails submitting to apostolic understanding of the Word.

The church has shown a certain ambivalence toward the apostles from its infancy. Paul's defense of himself to the Corinthians in 1 Corinthians 4:8–13 demonstrates this:

You are already filled, you have already become rich, you have become kings without us; and I would indeed that you had become kings so that we also might reign with you. For, I think, God has exhibited us apostles last of all, as men condemned to death; because we have become a spectacle to the world, both to angels and to men.

We are fools for Christ's sake, but you are prudent in Christ; we are weak, but you are strong; you are distinguished, but we are without honor. To this present hour we are both hungry and thirsty, and are poorly clothed, and are roughly treated, and are homeless; and we toil, working with our own hands; when we are reviled, we bless; when we are persecuted, we endure; when we are slandered, we try to conciliate; we have become as the scum of the world, the dregs of all things, even until now.

Even in the early church, believers had already begun challenging the crucial authority of the apostles, and theirs is an example we should not follow.

The book of Jude directs a polemic against leaders who lead the church astray, and he predicts that such leaders will multiply as the church ages. In verses 17–18, he prophesies:

But you, beloved, ought to remember the words that were spoken beforehand by the apostles of our Lord Jesus Christ, that they were saying to you, "In the last time there shall be mockers, following after their own ungodly lusts."

A mark of the end times, then, is a degeneration of the church into criticism of rather than obedience to apostolic teachings. Note also that this criticism is fueled by their immoral desires, which is certainly a mark of the modern church.

Whether or not you accept my understanding of leaving their "first love," the church today takes great exception with and is in fact ashamed of much of what the apostles taught. It has particularly targeted many of Paul's teachings. But if we reject his teachings on morality, on what basis do we accept the doctrine of justification by grace through faith, which he uniquely received from the Holy Spirit and laid out so systematically in the book of Romans? We cannot pick and choose. If the commandments are cultural, then so are the promises. And if the commandments are cultural, then our culture and not the Scripture is authoritative.

Paul says in 1 Corinthians 14:37–38, "If anyone thinks he is a prophet or spiritual, let him recognize that the things which I write to you are the Lord's commandment. But if anyone does not recognize this, he is not recognized." To repeat, the apostles encountered Jesus directly and have the mind of Christ, not us.

The Apostles Are Our Link to the Eternal Reality in the Heavenly Places

In the book of Ephesians, Paul repeats a phrase used nowhere else in the Scripture: "in the heavenly places." To what does this refer, and why is it important? The phrase is found in 1:3, 1:20, 2:6, 3:10 and 6:12. Without elaborating on all five verses, we learn that in some sense we are seated there with Christ (2:6), that God's wisdom is made known to other heavenly beings there through the church (3:10), and that the believer is in a battle against spiritual forces "in the heavenly places" (6:12).

These verses teach that the heavenly places are the spiritual realm, and Ephesians provides a glimpse of its eternal realities. Paul describes the church as John depicts her in Revelation 21—as being "built upon the foundation of the apostles and prophets, Christ Jesus Himself being the corner stone." He unfolds the mystery of her unity in Christ, which "in other generations was not made known to the sons of men, as it has now been revealed to His holy apostles and prophets in the Spirit" (Ephesians 2:20, 3:5). The apostles, then, along with the prophets, are the foundation of the church and the ones who have revealed the spiritual realities of the gospel to her.

As we discussed extensively in Chapter 2, "God, Knowledge, and Morality," the spiritual realm is the realm of causes, and our understanding of reality and our moral compass must be rooted there. Knowledge and morality were given to the church in the gospels and the apostolic writings, and because they are rooted in the changeless and eternal spiritual reality of Christ, they too are timeless and unchanging.

Believing and practicing what the apostles believed and practiced keeps us tethered to the spiritual realm of the heavenly places. By giving us the Holy Spirit, God gave us the means whereby to understand and imitate the apostles, for their teaching originated in the heavenly places. With respect to spiritual and moral truths, nothing can be added to or subtracted from the apostolic understanding of Christ.

To summarize: the apostles are God's gift to the church to freeze the eternal Christ in time. This is necessary because we live in a time-bound world that undergoes constant change. Apostolic teaching serves as the hermeneutic, or grid, through which we understand the scriptures. Their writings are not of this earth but originate in heaven itself. We leave our first love when we deviate from this heavenly truth as revealed by the apostles.

The ideologies we have discussed have all served the opposite purpose—to tear the church away from the eternal reality of Christ revealed through the apostles. The ideologies come not from the heavens, but from this earth; not from God, but from man. These philosophies stand contrary to the unchanging truths of God and are all the more difficult to withstand because they have woven themselves so deeply into our culture and cater so effectively to our sinful desires.

These ideologies (which for the purposes of simplicity, we will call secularism) have created a new religion with a novel feature—it denies the existence of the heavenly realm. As stated earlier, in the days of the pagan idols and temples, men understood four essential truths: a world exists beyond our senses, there is a wisdom that is higher than our own, our destiny is not in our own hands, and sacrifice for the sake of the divine is a necessary and central part of life.

Modern man no longer believes these truths. But men are incurably religious—all that has changed with secularism is the locus of our faith. Instead of serving pagan gods, the religion we practice now sacrifices individuals for the sake of mankind and has rejected divine morality and belief in an afterlife for the idolization of life on earth. The divinity we serve no longer resides in the gods, but in man himself.

We Are Engaged in a Spiritual Battle

The Bible, in contrast, contends that the heavenly places do in fact exist and that a battle for our souls is being waged there. In the final chapter of Ephesians, Paul teaches believers how we can win this battle:

> Finally, be strong in the Lord and in the strength of His might. Put on the full armor of God, that you may be able to stand firm against the schemes of the devil. For our struggle is not against flesh and blood, but against the rulers, against the powers, against the world forces of this darkness, against spiritual forces of wickedness in the heavenly places (Ephesians 6:10–12).

We cannot win the battle without the armor of God:

Therefore, take up the full armor of God, that you may be able to resist in the evil day, and having done everything, to stand firm. Stand firm therefore having girded your loins with truth, and having put on the breastplate of righteousness, and having shod your feet with the preparation of the gospel of peace; in addition to all, taking up the shield of faith with which you will be able to extinguish all the flaming arrows of the evil one. And take the helmet of salvation, and the sword of the Spirit, which is the word of God (Ephesians 6:13–17).

Though all of the armor is important, I want to discuss only three: the girding of truth, the breastplate of righteousness and the sword of the Spirit, which is the Word.

Note with me that in our spiritual battle, the first and foundational piece in the armor is to gird our loins with truth—in other words, knowledge. But as Pontius Pilate asked Jesus, "What is truth?" (John 18:38). His question accurately implies that man has achieved no consensus on the answer. How can we gird our loins with truth if we don't know what the truth is?

Answering this question correctly is particularly essential because Jesus tells us that the way to life is through the truth: "I am the way, and the truth, and the life; no one comes to the Father, but through Me" (John

14:6). Jesus Christ is the Truth, "in whom are hidden all the treasures of wisdom and knowledge" (Colossians 2:3), and we can only arrive at Truth through Him. Truth is the target of the secular religion, and their attack on truth has infected the church.

So which Jesus are we to embrace, the modern church's tolerant Jesus who leads us toward self-actualization and equity, or the Jesus of the apostles, who is the Lover of our souls and died to set us free from sin and death? The grid by which we view the scriptures and Jesus Christ must be the grid of the apostles because it alone is tethered to the heavenly places. Unless we maintain this lens, truth becomes an ever-shifting target molded by men rather than revealed by God. By embracing the culture, the church exchanges the truth of God for a lie (Romans 1:25).

The next piece of armor is the breastplate of righteousness—in other words, biblical morality. Our righteousness is grounded in the imputed righteousness of Christ; obedience to the New Testament commandments aligns the believer with that righteousness. Included in the commandments are both the positive commandments to love the Lord our God with all our hearts, souls, minds and strength and to love one another as Christ loved the church. But also included are the New Testament restrictions on morality, including prohibitions on sexuality outside of heterosexual marriage. The attack of cultural Marxism and secularism on biblical morality has effectively expunged the apostle's understanding of morality from the modern church. The modern church's morality is only slightly less progressive than that of our culture, and its revisions can only be resisted by returning to and obeying an apostolic understanding of the commandments.

The sword of the Spirit, which is the Word of God, provides the believer's final and only offensive weapon. Knowing the Book and its Author must be the goal of our lives, and understanding it as He intended, not as we desire it to be, must be our aim. This means we must know how to apply Scripture to all of life, including to how we think about these ideologies. Only by becoming students of the Word can we escape their deception.

The sword of the Word reveals the truth with which we must gird our loins and provides the moral framework for the righteousness with which we should shield our breast. By attacking biblical truth and righteousness, these ideologies have destroyed our ability to perceive truth and altered our morality. Rejecting the wisdom God granted the apostles, we have instead come to read the Word through secular eyes, thereby losing our only offensive weapon. We no longer know the truth or biblical morality because we do not believe the Word.

Taken together, these three pieces of armor were intended to perform an important function in the believer's life. By them, we learn two important truths about ourselves: 1) how easily we believe and even prefer the lies to the truth, and 2) how far short of God's righteousness we actually fall. God designed this process to produce that which sin produced in our first parents—shame. But we have lost our capacity for shame, even telling ourselves that shame itself is a sin. But this is not so. Godly shame brings a man to a place of brokenness, repentance, and dependence on God, and this state is the fertile soil in which Christ thrives.

The Great Physician came to heal the sick, but in our delusional fever, we are persuaded that we are well and reject His cure for the disease we do not believe we have. And so He moves on to the patient who knows all too well the extremity of his condition. Though the cure will cost him everything, such a man understands that without it he has nothing. Jesus promises, "Truly, truly, I say to you, unless a grain of wheat falls into the earth and dies, it remains by itself alone; but if it dies, it bears much fruit. He who loves his life loses it; and he who hates his life in this world shall keep it to life eternal" (John 12:24–25). Death to ourselves and the lies of this world remains the only cure for our otherwise terminal disease.

Two Opposing Truth Systems Compete for Our Souls

We cannot die to the lies of the world unless we can identify them. Two opposing truth systems battle for our souls, and learning to dissect the truth from the lies is critical to winning the war. Remember 2 Corinthians 10:3–5:

For though we walk in the flesh, we do not war according to the flesh, for the weapons of our warfare are not of the flesh, but divinely powerful for the destruction of fortresses. We are destroying speculations and every lofty thing raised up against the knowledge of God, and we are taking every thought captive to the obedience of Christ.

The two competing truth systems striving for our souls are the Bible, as understood by the apostles and tethered to the heavenly places, and the secular worldview, whose god is man. Again, for the sake of simplicity, I am conflating the ideologies we have just discussed to the term "secular worldview." The following table summarizes the critical divergences between these two opposing worldviews.

| Essential Differences Between Christianity and Secularism ||
Christianity	Secularism
Earthly life is a means to a spiritual end	Earthly life is an end in itself
Life is about spiritual reality underlying experience and the primacy of that reality	Life is about temporal conditions and their betterment
God spoke both the spiritual and natural worlds into existence	Man creates reality through his words (linguistic constructivism)
Our purpose on earth is to conform our souls to spiritual reality	Man conforms temporal reality to his will
Man is a free moral agent who can choose	Man is a victim of the laws of history and social and economic circumstances
Sin is individual, present in all, and is against God (man is the problem)	Sin is social and against classes of people, refected in unequal opportunity and outcomes (God is the problem)
Christ frees men from sin to be united with Him (goal is freedom)	Mankind can create material equality for all (goal is equity)
Contentment with respect to material things (I Tim. 6:8, Phil. 4:11-13)	Greed and covetousness with respect to material things
Love is the chief virtue and is gained through self-denial	Self-actualization and tolerace for others who self-actualize is a chief virtue, which is gained by acting on desires and passions
Each of us will endure judgment before Christ at the end of life (2 Cor. 5:10)	Believers have no eternal accountability (Church embraces this when it teaches that grace eliminates consequences for temporal behavior)

Most of these points we have discussed in detail already. To briefly summarize, secularism rejects God's morality and knowledge in favor of a humanistic redefinition of morality and reality. Its temporal worldview values tolerance of immorality (although not tolerance of opposing ideas) and tasks us with correcting inequity in our circumstances rather than the sin in our souls. God built this inherent inequity into life, and no one can fully rectify it this side of the grave. Instead, God expects us to allow the pain and unfairness of life to shape us into holy people whose reward waits in eternity. By focusing on inequity instead of freedom from sin, we are essentially telling God that our chief problem is the way He made the world rather than the sin in our souls.

Of course Christians are called to meet the temporal needs of those in distress. This is common Christian charity. Christ commands that His followers give to the poor, but that they do so in secret (Matthew 6:1–4) rather than as part of a public social justice program. Biblical love is an end in itself, but improving society is not. The aim of Christ's followers is spreading the gospel to redeem souls, and Christians have long understood that meeting physical needs offers a means to that end. For centuries in the West, the church was the sole provider of charity, and in fact the world has learned charity from the church. But too often today, the church meets physical needs but neglects sharing the gospel of Jesus Christ.

The Battle Will Be Won Through the Word

The third line in the comparative chart concerning words and their power requires a necessarily short elaboration. The world is constantly changing, and key to the force it exerts upon us are the words we use. Because words have such profound power to shape our concepts, and therefore our souls, the one who directs the conversation, by choosing the words or topics to be discussed, wields great authority. In the Garden, God controlled the conversation until Satan interjected. Since then, God has sought to redirect His people through the Bible. Richard Weaver noted in his book, *Ideas Have Consequences*, that "wisdom came to man in Christ . . . . Knowledge of the prime reality comes to man through the word; the word is a sort of deliverance from the shifting world of appearances."[1] The Word of God, the written expression of Christ, is an eternal truth that preserves the believer from the lies of the world.

But like Satan in the Garden, the secularists have hijacked the conversation. Crispin Sartwell notes how this linguistic constructivism functions in his article, "The 'Postmodern' Intellectual Roots of Today's Campus Mobs" in *The Wall Street Journal* (March 24, 2017): "That words have such power suggests that we can create a better world by re-narrating. But it also implies that we must control what people say and write and hear and read. If words make reality, then they are central."[2] The narrative that intellectuals began to tell following the Kennedy assassination has mesmerized our culture—and tragically, the church. Words shape our understanding of reality, and speech is increasingly being controlled by our enemies. We have the words of truth and dare not be ashamed of them.

Instead of the Christian view that we are to be transformed by the Living Word, who spoke the universe into being, the secularists are speaking a new world into being and transforming you and me in the process. They mock the Bible for teaching that God spoke creation into existence, while insisting that mere mortal men by their words can create a new world of their own. Over the last sixty years, their version of reality has grown increasingly despotic.

This new phenomenon makes resisting the secular assault on the authority of the scriptures all the more critical. We must return to the apostolic understanding of the Word of God if we are to win the spiritual battle for our souls. It is our only legitimate source of truth, and our only offensive weapon against the shroud of lies being woven around us.

The cost of following Christ has always been high. We in the modern West have paid little to follow Him, and as a result have lost the ability to see the plain truth of the Bible. The world is opposing Christ and His followers with increasing ferocity, and that cost to follow Him is about to go up for us. War is being waged against the truth of Christ, yet the modern church does not know how to biblically wage war. She has even forgotten the truth.

Conclusion

RECALL THE SCENARIO from the Introduction of a second century Christian man pointing out the idol's temple to his children. Now imagine a similar scenario today. To what building could you point? What concrete evidence of idolatry could your child observe to even formulate a question? I suggest that your children would be like me when I was a child during confirmation classes for my church. Upon learning of the commandment concerning idolatry, I quickly concluded that it posed little, if any, threat to me or the rest of the church.

We all face this challenge today. How can we identify idolatry that is abstract? Our idols reside not in a temple but in our hearts. Because our thinking is idolatrous, learning instead to think biblically is paramount.

Satan Tempts Us with Seduction Rather Than Reasoned Arguments

In the Garden of Eden, God laid the framework by which man must relate to Him: we must accept His revelation of truth, both moral and factual, by faith. Yet as the story illustrates, we have never wanted to relate to

God on His terms and have instead created idols we can control so we can become like God. First with the Jewish people and later with the church, God called His people out of idolatry into the perfect truth of His wisdom and commandments. Yet longing for autonomy, both Israel and the church synthesized the pure truths of God with the lies of idolatry. This policy is, in the words of the Bible, a discipline of delusion.

The modern church's idolatry has gone largely unnoticed because the ideologies we have discussed do not offer reasoned arguments. Reasoned arguments are unnecessary. Instead they appeal to the lust for autonomy lodged deep in our souls. They have not so much won a debate in the church as they have consummated a seduction.

But this seduction, far from being new, has been with us from the beginning. The Fall in Eden carries the same unmistakable fingerprint as today, expressed in the serpent's whisper, "Indeed, has God said, 'You shall not eat from any tree of the garden?'" The question is framed as an accusation against God, implying that He is not good and doesn't have our best interest at heart. It, too, is not a reasoned argument but a seduction, which speaks to our secret fear that God is not good and our secret ambition that we can replace Him.

The three temptations of our Lord by Satan in the wilderness replayed this same pattern. Satan successfully deceived Eve, but he failed to deceive Christ (Matthew

4:1–11). Jesus deflected the temptations by rejecting their premises and evaluating them instead from God's perspective as set forth in His Word.

This, then, must become the path for God's people to withstand temptation. As Jesus said to His disciples, "If you continue (abide) in My Word, then you are truly disciples of Mine; and you will know the truth, and the truth will make you free" (John 8:31–32). If we hope to fare better than Eve and escape deception, we must follow Christ's example by being biblical in our thinking and abiding in Him and His Word. Instead of thinking with the language and worldview of our culture, we must be transformed by the language and worldview of the "living and abiding word of God" (1 Peter 1:23).

Abiding in Christ requires emulating Him and examining the validity of our ideas, which necessitates understanding their origins and contents. By constantly questioning and reinterpreting the Bible, the refrain of the modern church has been, "Did God really say that?" We must turn this question on its head. *Did* God really tell us most of what the modern church believes? In many cases, the answer is no.

Instead, the wisdom of the world has become our source of truth. The wisdom of the world is by definition temporal in scope and ignorant of the eternal realities of God, His Word, and our souls. Together, science, secularism and cultural Marxism have generated a man-made system of knowledge and morality that minimizes the influence of the Bible, particularly the Bible as understood by the apostles, on God's people. They have done so by seducing, questioning, and replacing.

Science bestows great knowledge of the natural world. But because it ignores the spiritual reality behind the universe, the knowledge it provides is incomplete and often wrong. Technologies derived from it, such as the Internet and computer, flood us with temporal information, distracting us from the infinitely more important tasks of learning the eternal truths of Scripture and maturing our souls. The "progress" of scientific knowledge causes us to believe that our understanding of the Scripture should also "progress" and evolve, thereby departing from the apostles' understanding of Christ.

Secularism provides us with a temporal morality that conflicts sharply with the eternally-grounded morality of the Bible. It has deceived the church into believing that God will levy no consequences for temporal behavior in eternity, rendering happiness in this life, rather than holiness in preparation for the next, the goal of the modern church. For the secular Christian, this life is like Las Vegas—what happens here, stays here. We translate this temporal focus into how we "love" others, so that social justice rather than the Great Commission serves as our ministry to the world.

Cultural Marxism has completed the assassination of biblical morality in the church by attacking authority and promoting sexual immorality. In finally and fully toppling God's authority structure for the universe, it fulfills mankind's quest for autonomy foreshadowed in the Garden. By attacking the authority of the Bible, it has destroyed biblical morality and negated the Word as a source of authoritative, objective, revealed truth. All three ideologies ignore the existence of the spiritual realm and therefore the eternal, unchanging truths of Christ. By imbibing their ideas, eternal accountability, the development of the soul, and the Great Commission have become obsolete in the modern church.

The New Testament predicted the church would be tempted by falsehood just as Israel was. Peter prophesied, "But false prophets also arose among the people [of Israel], just as there will also be false teachers among you, who will secretly introduce destructive heresies, even denying the Master who bought them" (2 Peter 2:1). Among the hallmarks of such teachers, Peter noted they would "indulge the flesh in its corrupt desires and despise authority" (verse 10). These destructive heresies have targeted the authority of the apostolic understanding of the Bible and biblical morality, becoming our modern-day idols.

But the good news is that the antidote for our idolatry is already in our possession just as it was for Christ during His temptation. Today's church has an advantage that most of God's people, from the beginning of time until very recently, have not enjoyed—the Bible in the hands of the laity.

We Have No Excuse for Ignorance of the Truth

My parents performed a great service for me: they sent me to school, where I learned to read and write, and eventually, learned the rudiments of how to think. In the providence of God, I was born in the United States, where I have enjoyed the privilege of reading a Bible in my native tongue and the freedom to openly read and study it as much as I choose. I also possess access to more Bible study aids than were available in any of Europe's greatest medieval libraries. What bounty! What responsibility!

Many of you, whether born in the U.S. or not, have been similarly blessed. My point is that few of us have an excuse for not knowing what the Bible says. Through most of the church's history, the laity relied on the clergy to teach them the scriptures. Illiteracy and a lack of household Bibles required this. Thank the Lord for His faithful servants who ministered to the flock those many years. But things have changed.

I'm not saying faithful clerics no longer teach God's Word, but rather that the laity no longer has an excuse for not knowing if we are being taught the truth. But we, the laity, are sinful and lazy. We simply want someone to tell us what to think and do so that we can get on with our lives.

But we are spiritual beings, and the eternal is of greater importance than the temporal. The Word of God is the only food available for our souls. Furthermore, I contend that most of the Bible was written by and for laymen. True, Paul was professionally trained and played a centrally unique role in the early church. But all the other apostles and authors of the New Testament were laymen.

Thirty-five years ago, Walter A. Henrichsen and William N. Garrison published a book that proclaims, *Layman Look Up! God Has a Place for You.* Reclaim your heritage, layman. The Book is yours, a personal letter to you from the Lover of your soul. What an unspeakable gift God has given us—"things into which angels long to look" (1 Peter 1:12)! And there it sits on our bookshelves.

Each of us will give an account. When we stand before the Lord Jesus Christ in judgment, we will be alone. Our pastors, Sunday school teachers, small group leaders and elders will not be with us. When He asks why we so seldom studied His Word, how will we find the words to explain to Him that we had "bigger fish to fry" in this life?

This Present Life Is Shaping Our Eternity

The purpose of this life is to prepare us for an eternity with Jesus Christ, which means it is a test. Perhaps an analogy will help to understand the test.

The world is the *Titanic.* The ship struck the iceberg in Eden, and the blow was fatal. The ship is sinking, and nothing can stop it. But on the ship are lifeboats on which the name, "Jesus Christ, King of Kings and Lord of Lords," is written. Your mission and mine is to assist men, women and children, one soul at a time, from the *Titanic* onto the lifeboats.

We are tasked with two responsibilities on those lifeboats. First, we beckon those on the sinking ship to join us on our tiny but seaworthy crafts. And secondly, we learn to obey God and understand His ways. But in abandoning the *Titanic* for those lifeboats, we bring with us the ways of the *Titanic* and its ideologies. Refuting those evil ways lies at the heart of our homeward sojourn, that we may emulate the culture of the new world for which we are bound.

To repeat, the world is the *Titanic*, and this world is built upon ideas—ideas conceived by Satan, the father of lies. Because he is prince of this world, God granted him permission to deceive men with his lies and to build our world upon them. But the lifeboats are imprinted with the plain truth of Jesus Christ and the Bible. The *Titanic* expresses the wisdom of the world, and the lifeboats the wisdom of God. And they cannot be mixed. Only one of these vessels will carry us safely home. We foolishly believe that we can live with one foot on each at our own convenience. But this is a lie born in hell.

Separating the wisdom of the world from the wisdom of God is not easy. My hope is that this book will be of some small aid to you in this endeavor. Do not take my word for it, but be like the Bereans, who "were more noble-minded than those in Thessalonica, for they received the word with great eagerness, examining the Scriptures daily, to see whether these things were so" (Acts 17:11). God knows those who belong to Him and how to communicate with them. As Jesus says, "Everyone who is of the truth hears My voice." (John 18:37)

And all the while, the lifeboats are tossed about on stormy seas, tempting us to return to the seemingly more stable *Titanic*. The allure of spending our lives rearranging the deck chairs on that ill-fated ship is very great, and the world and much of the church will commend us for so doing. But lifeboats are aptly named. In a shipwreck, only those on the lifeboats will live.

Endnotes

Introduction

1. William Kilpatrick, *Why Johnny Can't Tell Right from Wrong: Moral Illiteracy and the Case for Character Education* (New York: Simon & Schuster, 1992) p. 100.

2. George Will, "When Liberals Became Scolds," *Washington Post* (Oct. 9 2013).

3. Ibid.

Chapter 1

1. Bill Lind, "The Origins of Political Correctness," www.academia.org/the-origins-of-political-correctness, accessed 09/19/17.

Chapter 4

1. Whittaker Chambers, *Witness* (Washington, DC: Gateway Editions, 1952) p. 9.

Chapter 5

1. Richard Weaver, *Ideas Have Consequences* (London: University of Chicago Press, 1948) p. 4.

2. Ibid.

3. Stephen L. Goldman, "Science Wars: What Scientists Know and How They Know It." *The Great Courses* (Chantilly: The Teaching Company, 2006) p. 15.

Chapter 6

1. Anthony Daniels, preface to *Last Exit to Utopia: The Survival of Socialism in a Post-Soviet Era* by Jean-Francois Revel (New York: Encounter Books, 2000) p. xxii.

Chapter 7

1. Michael Walsh, *The Devil's Pleasure Palace: The Cult of Critical Theory and the Subversion of the West* (New York: Encounter Books, 2015) p. 3.

2. Nikolas Lobkowicz, "Marxism as the Ideology of Our Age," http://www.leaderu.com/truth/1truth13.html, accessed 9/19/17.

3. Walsh, p. 85.

4. Lind, Op Cit.

5. Gerald L. Atkinson, "What Is the Frankfurt School (And Its Effects Upon America)," http://www.wvwnews.net/story.php?id=8183 (August 1, 1999), accessed 09/19/17.

6. Bill Flax, "Deconstructing President Obama's Strange Stance on Israel," *Forbes* (June 2, 2011), www.forbes.com/forbes/welcome/?toURL=https://www.forbes.com/sites/billflax/2011/06/02/deconstructing-president-obamas-strange-stance-on-israel/&refURL=https://search.yahoo.com/&referrer=https://search.yahoo.com/, accessed 09/19/17.

7. Lind, p.3.

8. Walsh, p. 49.

9. Walsh, p. 42.

10. Lind, Op Cit.

11. Paul Kengor, *Takedown* (Washington, DC: WND Books, 2015).

12. Walsh, p. 70.

13. Atkinson, pp. 2-3.

14. Lind, p. 5.

15. Atkinson, p. 3.

16. David Horowitz, *Radical Son: A Generational Odyssey* (New York: Touchstone Books, 1997), p. 112.

17. Chambers, p. 9.

Chapter 8

1. Weaver, p. 11.

2. Crispin Sartwell, "The 'Postmodern' Intellectual Roots of Today's Campus Mobs," *The Wall Street Journal* (March 24, 2017).

CPSIA information can be obtained
at www.ICGtesting.com
Printed in the USA
BVOW06s2246240118
506172BV00006B/594/P